Encyclopedia of American Cat Breeds

by Meredith Wilson

Front cover:
Beachmor Jessica, a Scottish Fold female, owned and bred by Mr. and Mrs. F.M. Dreifuss. Photo by Florence M. Harrison.

Back cover:
Top, left: Grand Champion Kidar's Silver Pearl, a Persian, owned by Bettijane Myjak. *Top, right:* Two Somali kittens, left, L'Air de Rauch's Boo, owned by Mr. and Mrs. John Moore; right, L'Air de Rauch Rocky Raccoon of Foxtail, owned by Patricia Warren. Photo by Manny Greenhaus. *Center, left:* A Ragdoll kitten, owned by Mr. Morris Epstein. *Bottom, left:* Persian kittens, left, Double Grand Champion Willow Lane Precious; right, Willow Lane Little Bit, owned by Isabel Roberts. Photo by Blair Studio. *Bottom, right:* Double Champion Mor-Ace's Bettie Joe, a brown tabby Maine Coon, owned by Anthony Morace. Photo by Kevin T. Sullivan.

Frontispiece:
Mrs. Leslie Buckingham's Sun Dance Raisin Kane of Kyat, an Abyssinian bred by Donna Coss. Photo by Buckingham.

ISBN 0-87666-855-4

Distributed in the U.S. by T.F.H. Publications, Inc., 211 West Sylvania Avenue, P.O. Box 427, Neptune, N.J. 07753; in England by T.F.H. (Gt. Britain) Ltd., 13 Nutley Lane, Reigate, Surrey; in Canada to the book store and library trade by Clarke, Irwin & Company, Clarwin House, 791 St. Clair Avenue West, Toronto 10, Ontario; in Canada to the pet trade by Rolf C. Hagen Ltd., 3225 Sartelon Street, Montreal 382, Quebec; in Southeast Asia by Y.W. Ong, 9 Lorong 36 Geylang, Singapore 14; in Australia and the South Pacific by Pet Imports Pty. Ltd., P.O. Box 149, Brookvale 2100, N.S.W., Australia; in South Africa by Valiant Publishers (Pty.) Ltd., P.O. Box 78236, Sandton City, 2146, South Africa; Published by T.F.H. Publications, Inc., Ltd., The British Crown Colony of Hong Kong.

Contents

ACKNOWLEDGMENTS

My sincere thanks go to the following people, whose help has made this book possible. Without their help many of the breeds would be sorely lacking in the information that is provided in this book. These people have given of their knowledge, their time and their enthusiasm to see such a book published. Words of thanks to them can never be enough.

A special "Thank You" goes to Mr. Raymond Smith, publisher of *Cats Magazine*, for his time and comments. He was kind enough to read the manuscript, and I appreciate most sincerely his interest and his help.

A special thank you goes also to my "editors", each a specialist in a given breed, who took time to read each breed section and to comment on what I had already put together. Their help is very much appreciated. Their names appear in italics below accompanied by their breed specialty.

It is my hope that in thanking all these people I do not miss anyone. In such a large endeavor it is difficult to hit the mark every time, but it is my hope to thank every person who helped to make this book possible.

To all of you, a heartfelt thanks!

Helen Gamon-Chartreux; *Jean Smelt*-Balinese; Lydia Messier-British Shorthair; *Sandy Kaiser*-Sphynx; Evelyn Piriano-Bombay; *Pat Taylor*-Bombay; *Thomas and Virgina Torio*-Turkish Angora; Janet Hershey and Jill Archibald-Egyptian Mau.

Donna Coss-Abyssinian; Brooklyn Public Library; *Cats Magazine; Cat Fancy; Cat World; Salle Wolf Peters*-Scottish Fold; Patricia Nell Warren-Somali; *Madalyn Dakin*-Tonkinese; Dian Jensen-Tonkinese; *Jane Cox*-Oriental Shorthair.

Erica Mueller-Oriental Shorthair; *Jean Krysuk*-Egyptian Mau; *Daphne Negus*-Korat; Esther Epstein-Korat; Olga Lewis-assorted information but mostly the Colorpoint Shorthair; Marge Gray-Abyssinian; Elsie Fisher-Birman; *Harriet Rindfleisch*-Birman; Helen Smith-Balinese.

Shirley Keenan-Egyptian Mau; *Elree Kellogg*-Manx; *Judith Shaw*-Manx; Carol and Mary Demars-Tonkinese; *Mrs. Harry Mauge*-Somali; *Tony and Lee Morace*-The Maine Coon; Bettijane Myjak-British Shorthair; *Laurie Stevens*-The Himalayan; Princess Natalie Troubetskoye-Egyptian Mau; *Donna Fuller*-Russian Blue. *Kathy Rohrer*-British Shorthair; Mrs. Bev Reedy-Oriental Shorthair; Martha Underwood-Sphynx; Ann Costa-Sphynx; *Bernadette Madden*-Rex; *Jeanne Singer*-Siamese; *Anne E. Bickman*-American Wirehair; *Dr. Rosemonde Peltz*-American Wirehair; *Paul and Dorothy Minner*-American Shorthair; *Jane Skeels*-Japanese Bobtail; *Jack and Barbara Collins*-Colorpoint Shorthair; *Mary DePew*-Burmese; Laura Dayton-Ragdoll; Anne Baker-Ragdoll; Michael and Barbara Hodits-Japanese Bobtail; Blair Wright-Longhaired Manx; Carolyn McLaughlin-Japanese Bobtail, Turkish Angora and Exotic Shorthair.

Jean Laux (*Cats Magazine*) a special thanks for breed club addresses, but mostly for encouragement and cheer over all these years of my writing. Bless you!

Jane Perkins-for back copies of magazines without which much information would not be included. Thanks, Jane.

AUTHOR'S COMMENT

This book was undertaken with great interest, curiousity and, as with all of my writing, with great enjoyment. My hope has been to cover some thirty breeds and to cover them to the best of my research ability. All research is based on the material available and on the help of those people instrumental in working with these breeds over the years. With newer breeds enthusiasm is greater, and information is less likely to become fogged. Because their inception is new, there is little disagreement about history and origins, although there may well be differences in breeding practices. The history of older breeds is often mere speculation on the part of myself and the references I used, because such breeds go back hundreds of years.

We in the United States who have chosen cats as pets or for a hobby, whether to breed or show or both, have a large number of breeds from which to choose. The purpose of this book is to show what breeds are on the scene today. However, it should be remembered by those who breed these cats and read this book that we are also a country with more than one registry and certainly more than one point of view. There are eight associations in the United States and one in Canada, and the latter country has been instrumental in this book and thus should be included.

No breed was ever accepted with every association at the same time—if indeed it was recognized by all associations at a given time. Some breeds are accepted in all associations, others are recognized by a few and not others, while other breeds are accepted in one manner in one association and in another manner in others. I have used CFA standards wherever a given breed is accepted by that registry. I have turned to other associations for other breeds not accepted to date by CFA. Readers should recognize that though their association or associations do not accept a given breed or color, it is this writer's obligation to present it if it has been accepted by a legitimate registry in this country and is being currently shown. As author I do not choose to take sides on any issues of where cats should be judged (in color classes or breed classes), nor do I wish to decide which colors of a breed should be recognized and which should not be. I am presenting the breeds and colors available to the American cat person be he a cat fancier or a simple cat lover. For readers who feel strongly that any point about a breed was not covered in the light they see their breed, please realize that every breed club was approached in one manner or another to obtain information. That was the time to step forward and be heard.

My own feelings on this book are strong. Three years of research have gone into it and to my knowledge it is the only book that covers these breeds in total and which presents American breeds using American standards and American illustrations. The pictures portray the best of the best in this country. This book is an American Breed Book! I have learned much doing the book and find each breed a unique and lovely animal in its own right. Where it was possible, history has been provided; where it was possible, breeding studies have been supplied—and all information available to me was provided for the reader to make for an interesting chapter on each breed without doing an entire separate book on each breed.

It must be remembered, too, that new breeds and new colors of established breeds will be accepted even as this book goes to the press. Some cats may enter new classes of competition, as the cat fancy is an everchanging world and no book can tell more than what is happening at the time of the writing.

My only hope is that you will enjoy the book. These are your cats!!!

About This Book

For thoroughness and ease in reading, the book falls into two separate sections. The first deals with each individual breed of cat, its history, the development of the breed, pioneer breeders, cat personality, commentary on structure and accepted colors. The second part of the book deals with the allowable colors for each breed. Because cats have been happily heir to a veritable feline rainbow of coat colors, organization and regulation of these has to have been done with the consideration that a cat's coat is its glory. With this in mind, a wide range of solid colors, patterns and color combinations are admitted in the standard. Many breeds are accepted in many of the same colors, some breeds are admitted in some of these plus some others, and several occur in only one or a few colors unique to their breeds.

In the first part of her narrative, Miss Wilson refers to a number of standard-setting organizations for pedigreed cats. The following are identifications of those bodies:

ACFA — American Cat Fancier's Association
ACA — American Cat Association
CCA—Canadian Cat Association
CFA — Cat Fanciers Association, Inc.
CFF — Cat Fanciers Federation
CCFF — Crown Cat Fanciers Federation, Inc.
NCFA — National Cat Fanciers Association, Inc.
UCF — United Cat Federation

Grand Champion Abyiat's Saskia of Gallantree, a ruddy Abyssinian female, owned by Ron and Judy Bauer. The breeder was Mrs. Brenda H. Garnett. Photo by Jensen.

Abyssinian

From the time that the Aby arrived on the scene in the cat fancy, much has been written on its ancestry. The English were the first to see and work with this breed. They are to be credited with first bringing it to the cat fancy and then exporting this beautiful animal to America. Some have called this cat the Child of the Gods, believing it to be descended from the cats of ancient Egypt that were worshipped there more than four thousand years ago. Others felt that the cat resembled and was related to the small wild cats of North Africa and thus had its origin in the jungles of Africa. Others, less inclined to these stories, believed the Aby to be a descendant of the British Domestic Tabby—a breeder's creation—the result of time and devotion to a strict breeding program which developed the ticking that so distinguishes the breed. Those who felt strongly about the legend of the Aby put their feelings into writing and brought forth publications attempting to trace this breed's ancestry. In England, H.C. Brooke published *The Abyssinian Cat*, which was followed, also in England, by Helen and Sidney Denham's *Child of the Gods*. In America the study of the Aby's origin became the effort of Aida Zanetti, Elinor Dennis and Mary E. Hantzmon, who published *The Journey From the Blue Nile* for the United Abyssinian Club. All these people had a firm belief that the Aby had its origin long ago in a far away place. There is something to be said for both theories.

The Aby could very well be the Egyptian cat which was worshiped and held sacred. Its body type and the facial structure, in fact the entire shape of the cat with its erect ears, have much the same look as the cats seen in bronzes and drawings dating back to ancient Egypt. Such a theory is not in contradiction to the theory that the Aby is also a descendant of an African wild cat. It has generally been believed that the domestic feline once wandered out of the jungle and was gentled by man. It should be noted that

11

Grand Champion and Champion Sun Dance Sarva, owned by Donna Coss and Jack Ours. The breeder was Donna Coss. Photo by Donna Coss.

the small wild cats of northern Africa have much in common with the Aby and could indeed be its ancestor. Descriptions of various species include references to a color of light gray, yellow or even slightly ruddy. It was supposed to have carried markings which were faint stripes, broken; they were not tabby-like but more like a ticking. One description notes that its fur was similar to that of the rabbit, with black at the tips, while other descriptions include a similar color to the extremities and belly and even a long black-tipped tail. The next question that comes to mind is how a "Child of the Gods of Egypt" came to be called the Abyssinian. Should the cat not have been called The Egyptian? To understand this is to investigate the history and the area from which this animal is believed to have come. The cat is believed to have made its way from the Nile. The Nile indeed ties in both the Abyssinian background of this cat and its claim to being of royal Egyptian blood. The Nile flows as the Blue Nile from Ethiopia, as it is known today, to the White Nile and then north to Egypt. Ethiopia is the modern name for what was then known as Abyssinia. The histories of Abyssinia and Egypt were long linked in history, and thus what was common to one could well be common to the other. Indeed, the Abyssinian cat could have been found in Abyssinia as well as in Egypt.

Proof of this argument seems to rest in a cat that recently came to the United States directly from Ethiopia. It was born in 1957 in Addis Ababa out of a domestic mother and a semi-wild father. The cat's name was Smokey P., and he lived in Massachusetts with his owners, Mr. and Mrs. William Maguire. He is believed to have looked like his father and to have been a true Aby, thus deserving of the name of the place from which he came and of the lineage of these cats—that of being the descendant of the sacred cats of Egypt.

A basketful of charm: Graymar Timothy, an Abyssinian kitten owned and bred by Mrs. John E. Gray. Photo by C. Harrison.

Van Dyke Abi-Aurene of Sun Dance, a female, owned by Gerald and Donna Coss. The breeder was Lila Rippy. Photo by Larry Levy.

There is no evidence to back up the theory that the Aby is the work of English breeders who transformed a British Domestic Tabby into the Aby, a new breed. The body structure of the two breeds is different, and the markings are greatly different. Also, no records exist of such breedings.

Whatever its heritage the Aby, once discovered, became loved. It was first brought to England in 1868 about the time of the end of the Abyssinian War. The first cat's name is reported to have been Zula; it was believed to have been imported by a Mrs. Barrett-Lennard. There is no firm evidence of this; however, soldiers returning from battle in other lands often bring home what they consider unique, and the Aby could well have come to England at this time in this manner. In England the cat was first listed as a separate breed and by the name Abyssinian in 1882. By 1900 the name was changed to Ticked or British Ticks. It is also believed that they were called Bunny Cats (due to their similarity of coat) or Cunnys.

There were many early enthusiasts who worked with the cat in England. The Stud Book of the National Cat Club shows that in 1896 the first Aby registration took place. The first two Abys registered were bred by a Mr. Swinyard and were called Sedgemere Bottle (born 1892), and Sedgemere Peaty (born 1894). A Miss Carew-Cox, who was an early and avid breeder, had a female called Fancy Free and a male cat named Aluminum. In 1907 this pair produced a male called Aluminum II, who would be one of the first Abyssinians to be exported to the United States. Aluminum II and Salt, a female also born in 1907 and also bred by Miss Carew-Cox, were acquired by Miss Jane Cathcart and were the first Abys imported into the United States. These cats were shown in Boston in 1909 by their owner. Years passed before new imports were made, but in 1934 a Mrs. Gardiner Fiske of Boston imported from England a pair of kittens that had been bred by Major Sydney Woodiwiss, who was a prominent Aby breeder of the time. The cats were named Woodroofe Anthony and Woodroofe Ena. The male was later altered, but the female was taken by Mrs. Virginia Cobb of Massachusetts and became Woodroofe Ena of Newton. In 1936 Ena was leased to Mrs. Martin Metcalf and Miss Mary Hantzmon. They were two prominent Aby breeders in this country and helped establish the breed. They proceeded to import Champion Ras Seyum from England (also from Major Sydney Woodiwiss) in 1937 and then in 1938 imported two more cats from another prominent English breeder. Mrs. Claire Basnett of Croham cattery sent these two ladies Djer-Mer Croham Justina and Djer-Mer Croham Isana. In the meantime the first Aby born in America was born in 1935 and was named Addis Ababa.

This writer would not attempt to list all those who followed suit breeding and importing the Aby to bring it to its popularity today as a show cat and as a breed. To name a few would be to take the chance of missing one, but for those who work with this breed the cattery names are prominent in all good pedigrees, and the results are seen in the show ring.

Right, top: Grand Champion Sun Dance Monisa of Eairywood, owned by Donna Coss and Bela Kertay. The cat was bred by Donna Coss. Photo by Donna Coss.
Right, bottom: Gallantree's Kristy, a Grand Champion and Quad. Champion. She is breeder-owned by Ron and Judy Bauer. Photo by Curtis.
Below: Grand Champion Thieroff's Flash Farkel. He is breeder-owned by Elaine Thieroff. Photo by Elaine Thieroff.

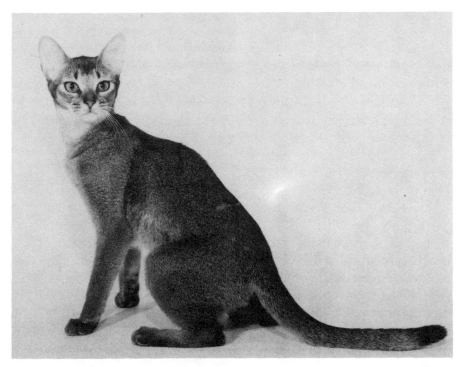

Amadear Hot Pepper of Amichka, owned by Mrs. Michelle Savickas. Breeders were Dr. and Mrs. Duane E. Young. Photo by Bryan Allen.

From those who own Abys I have learned that they are highly intelligent and very easy to train. Many claim they can be taught to walk on leash, to sit up and even to shake hands. They are reported to have sweet personalities, a sense of humor and a love of people. They are usually either asleep or on the go. They are built for agility and move quickly. They are fairly quiet, and their voices have been described as a bird-like trill or bell-like with a chirping when they wish to talk, especially to their babies. As mothers they are fierce and very vocal in defense of their young.

Characteristic of the Aby is its ticking. Because of the ticking it has been often referred to as the Bunny Cat, though the wild rabbit is not sound to the skin in color but rather has a greyish fur near the skin. The Aby, in contrast, has a bright color whether it be ruddy or red. The ticking is caused by black or dark brown (chocolate in the case of the red Aby) tips to each hair; the best representatives of the breed have this color on each hair. There are two colors. The ruddy will have a color that is ruddy brown with dark brown or black ticking. The red, a dilution of the ruddy, has a coat color of glowing red with a ticking of chocolate. Newborn ruddy kittens are born ruddy in coloring, and the tip of the tail and top of the head will show black often extending down the back. Red kittens will have no black at all but will be red with the tip of the tail and top of the head chocolate. A ruddy kitten will have darker nose leather and footpads. A red kitten will have pink nose leather and footpads. Ticking begins to show at from four to six weeks. It can take up to a year longer before the mature coat color is obtained.

The Abyssinian is a medium-size cat, but despite its delicate and dainty look it is a solid cat with good muscle tone. The head is a wedge that is slightly rounded but without any flat planes. There is a gentle contour to the browline, the cheeks and the profile giving it a sweet look—never severe. There is a slight rise from the bridge of the nose to the forehead with good width between the ears. This extends to the swanlike arch of the neck. The ears on the Aby are large and alert and moderately pointed and broad. They are set as though the cat were listening, and the Aby is known for being alert and aware of its surroundings. Its eyes are particularly interesting. They are expressive, large and almond-

Amara Ms. Annie Oakley, owned and bred by Bob and Lorna Malinen. Photo by Laurence Alberton.

shape. The eye color can be greenish gold or hazel but should be rich and deep in tone. The eyes are rimmed in black; a dark line extends up and out from the corner of the eye, giving a pixieish look. These "clown markings" should be prominent. The Aby has a medium body that is neither cobby nor svelte like the Oriental type cat. Its legs are slim and fine-boned with small, oval paws. To add to its alert look the cat, when standing, looks as though it were standing on tip-toes. The tail is thick at the base, moderately long and tapering to a tip. The Aby's coat is short, but soft and fine to the touch. It is also dense and resilient and should spring back when a finger is pushed across the coat against the lay of the coat. It is short in length but long enough to accommodate two or three bands of ticking.

The Abyssinian is accepted in two colors only, the Red and the Ruddy.

Opposite:
Top: R.M. Grand Champion and Champion Sun Dance Saffari of Zeni. Breeder-owners are Donna Coss and Inez Savage. Photo by Donna Coss.
Bottom: Triple Champion Sun Dance Ciara. Breeder-owner is Donna Coss. J'Sen's Photo.

Grand Champion Min-Dees Taglito Jason of Silver Myne, a silver tabby American Shorthair. He is owned by Rosemary Kendrick and was
bred by Peggy G. Minner. Photo by Fritz.

American Shorthair

When the American Shorthair came to this country it came continuing a tradition that has followed the cat from early Egyptian times to the present. When man first domesticated the cat he quickly found that "cat" and he had a common enemy in the rodents that destroyed crops and food supplies. As many cats in ancient times and later in Europe were kept for protection of food supplies as were kept for pets. The cat has often earned its way in the world, and in many instances value was attributed to this animal in monetary terms based on the cat's ability to be a mouser. It was often unlawful to harm the animal—not only because of religious beliefs but also because of its value as a worker.

European cats were the ancestors of those that were to come across the seas with the founders of this country. They came as pets, but they also came as workers. On ship their mousing ability protected the ship's stores from mice. As the Puritans established their homes and then spread out over the land, their cats went along as companions and as workers in the family units. Cats protected the first Americans from rats, mice and other rodents and provided companionship at the same time. These cats were free-roaming, and thus they were free-breeding. They certainly were not bred for their hunting ability, as this came naturally to them, and the form of their bodies seem to fit this task to a tee.

The American Shorthair today is much the same as its original state—it is a natural cat suited to a natural environment. It has always been known for its stamina, its intelligence, its ruggedness, its ability to survive and its hunting ability. Also, because of the breed's free-roaming and free-breeding patterns, the colors of its representatives became varied, and their bodies adapted more and more to their work and environment. There is no mystery to this breed. It is a natural. It came to this country as did the first

A body shot of Rosemary Kendrick's silver tabby, Grand Champion Min-Dees Taglito Jason of Silver Myne. Breeder was Peggy G. Minner. Photo by Fritz.

Americans—not truly American at all, but of European ancestry—but once here it became an American cat sharing hearth and home with the first Americans.

When the cat fancy began there was little interest shown in the American Shorthair, since interest turned immediately to cats imported from abroad. These were the unique, the new, the lovely, exotic and rare breeds. It was a long time before the American Shorthair was looked upon as a show possibility. Finally, in the 1890's, the shorthaired cat in America, our own breed, was looked upon as a show possibility, and it is believed it was at the first cat show at Madison Square Garden. It was simply called the Shorthair at the time.

This brings us to a discussion of this cat's name, which varies from association to association. Was it a Domestic Shorthair? An American Shorthair? An American Domestic Shorthair? Whatever, it has adapted to a new country and a new environment in the same way its owners did, and it can be easily distinguished from other Shorthaired breeds. It is different from the British Shorthair, the Exotic Shorthair and the Oriental Shorthair. It is certainly "domestic," but so are all other purebred cats. It is surely a purebred, since its acceptance into the cat fancy has earned it a standard of excellence to which breeders breed. So the name is American Shorthair, a distinct breed that had its birth as we know it here in America.

Another question that comes to mind when showing an American Shorthair or owning one is this: how does the American Shorthair differ from the common alley cat? Indeed, the American Shorthair comes the closest to looking like what most spectators have at home. When a spectator stops and remarks that the American Shorthair looks like a cat should, he knows what he is talking about. The ancestors of our American Shorthairs indeed had their origin as pets and workers, and the average cat lover sees this as a natural breed that is familiar to him. What is the dif-

Chin Hills Hellenic Prize, a brown classic tabby. She is owned and was bred by Roger and Rochelle Horenstein.

ference? American Shorthairs are indeed purebred and have been bred selectively to a standard that has maintained what is lovely and natural about this breed. Is it possible, then, to find a cat fitting the standard among a litter of strays? Some would say yes, and for this reason it is possible in some registries to register such cats and their parents and thus start a foundation stock for a new line of American Shorthairs. What is the criterion? The standard! If the cat can meet the standard, then it can compete and breed its qualities into its offspring. In the beginning, when the breed was new to the fancy, this was done freely, since breeders had to start somewhere. From the cats they found roaming free they worked toward the standard they had set, always striving for the American Shorthair that reflected the natural breed we see in the showring today. The grands we see in the showring reflect the success that breeders have had. We must realize that the British Shorthair indeed has its ancestors and cousins roaming the streets of London, just as the Chartreux has its free-roaming cousins over the French countryside and the Abyssinian today still breeds freely and is valuable in its natural state *sans* pedigree in Africa.

The recorded history of the American Shorthair in this country goes back to the first show in which it was entered at Madison Square Garden and to the first registry, the American Cat Fanciers Association. Cat Fanciers Association stud books show us something of interest about the beginning of this breed. The first Shorthair to be registered was an import from England, an orange tabby male named Belle of Bradford, imported by Miss Jane Cathcart and bred by a Mr. Kuhnel. This was about 1900. The second cat registered was also an import; named Pretty Correct, it was a silver tabby male imported by Miss Cathcart and bred by a Mrs. Collingwood in England. How were these English cats—probably British Shorthairs—to become the foundation of American Shorthair stock? Again, there was a standard and there was an open registration, so cats of unknown parentage could be registered. The next Shorthair was such a cat, again registered by Miss Cathcart. He was a smoke male born 1904; called Buster Brown, he was registered with unknown parentage. Thus, a true American Shorthair had been registered, and many more were to follow. The colors were varied and still are among the American Shorthairs shown, but the silver tabby has always been a favorite

Grand Champion Apache Taglito Jeffords, a black smoke American Shorthair male. He is owned by Dorothy H. Minner and was bred by Alayne Poeltl.

and a hard cat to beat in the showring for its beauty. From these beginnings breeders worked in all the color areas to perfect the American Shorthair as we know it.

What exactly was the breeder breeding for? Having owned an American Shorthair, I believe I know. This is a truly natural breed in both disposition and body conformation. There are no extremes to this cat. It flows smoothly with nothing suggesting a slide toward the cobby, the short, the Oriental, the delicate, the exotic. It is natural. Moderation in all ways best describes this breed, and those who have faithfully served the American Shorthair over the years have bred strictly for that moderation of all its aspects, having nothing to do with any extreme, however small. They leave that up to other breeds and leave the American Shorthair pure and natural.

Owning American Shorthairs is a joy. They have a natural personality, neither sleepy nor overly excited. They seem to take life in stride and above all are intelligent and independent. They also are loving and very gentle with adults and children. The cat can be

Grand Champion Tabb-I-Ville Tippecanoe, a silver tabby. He was bred by Mr. and Mrs. Lawrence Clayton Smith and is owned is Myrna Y. Ford. Photo by Everett E. Putney.

Grand Champion Chin Hills Magic Tone. This bi-color female is owned and was bred by Roger and Rochelle Horenstein.

clever and can be a tease. It has a tremendous sense of balance and great agility. It is a hunter, even in the house, attacking even a piece of paper as though it were the real thing. They tend to use their paws a lot and well, and their touch is gentle and soft as a velvet glove. Their cry is neither demanding nor meek—it is simply a request put directly. American Shorthairs are beautiful animals with great grace and dignity. I have been told they make excellent breeders—again, a tribute to their natural breeding. Their instincts are intact and good. It is a joy to own one, and they make excellent companions.

The American Shorthair has a large head with a pleasant, full-cheeked face that is just slightly longer than wide. Its nose is medium in length, not long or short, and is of uniform width with a gentle curve. The muzzle is square; the chin is firm and well developed, while the neck continues the strong look and is muscular and medium in length. Already it is easy to see a cat that is moderate in all aspects and gently works its component parts into a harmonious whole. The ears are medium in size and slightly rounded at the tip; they are set wide, but not too open at the base. The cat's eyes are round and wide and set wide apart, giving an open look to the bright and alert face. The body is medium to

Above: Head shot of Grand Champion Min-Dees Taglito Jason, a silver tabby.
Below: Champion Chin Hills Agamemnon, a brown mackerel tabby, owned by Roger and Rochelle Horenstein.

large. It is well knit and powerful, with a well developed chest and heavy shoulders. Obviously, this cat makes for a strong hunter. Its legs are medium in length, firmly boned and muscled, built for easy movement and for jumping. Its paws are firm, full and rounded with heavy pads. The tail is medium long in keeping with the body, heavy at the base and tapering to a blunt end. The coat is short, thick, even and hard in texture. All in all the cat is strong, well knit, moderate in all ways and built for a rugged life, showing strength and stamina and above all a pleasant over-all look.

The American Shorthair is accepted in the blue-eyed white, the odd-eyed white, the copper-eyed white, the blue, black, red, cream, chinchilla, shaded silver, shell cameo, shaded cameo, black smoke, blue smoke, cameo smoke, classic and mackerel silver tabby, red tabby, brown tabby, cream tabby, cameo tabby, tortoiseshell, calico, dilute calico, blue-cream and bi-color.

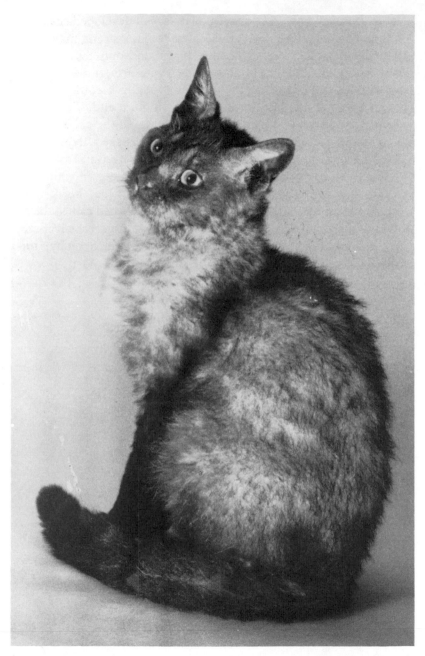

Heatherwood's Short Circuit, an American Wirehair, owned by Anne Bickman.

American Wirehair

Courtesy of Rosemonde S. Peltz, M.D. and Anne Bickman

Occasionally in nature two like creatures produce offspring quite unlike themselves. Such a genetic mutation resulted in the American Wirehaired cat.

The American Wirehair is the most recent mutation to occur among the domestic cats of the United States. More significantly, it is the only mutation in the cat that has not, as yet, appeared anywhere else in the world.

This mutation originated in a male kitten born in a litter of farm cats in Verona, New York, in 1966. Mrs. John O'Shea acquired the original mutant, ultimately named Council Rock Farm Adam of Hi-Fi, and his female littermate, Tip-Toe. At maturity these two cats were bred and produced four kittens, two of which were wirehaired.

Several people became involved in the project. Within a few years, breeding stock went to Mr. and Mrs. William Beck of Maryland, Dr. Rosemonde Peltz of Georgia and Mr. Robert Bradshaw of Illinois. Through a series of selective breedings, the American Wirehair became established as a breed, and cats were placed with Mr. Conway Lewis of Canada, Ms. Elke Frehse of Germany and Mrs. Anne Bickman and Mr. Charles Hutto of Georgia.

The American Wirehair is a unique cat, distinguished from all others by a change in the guard hairs of the coat. Instead of being smooth and tapering, the guard hairs are crimped along the shaft and hooked at the end. The coat, which was quite sparse in the early representatives of the breed, has been developed into a thick, coarse, resilient coat which is not unlike sheep's wool. The mutation is dominant and non sex-linked.

From its free-roaming ancestors, the American Wirehair has in-

Above: Chinquapin's Circuit Breaker. This copper eyed white male is owned by Karen A. Votava. Breeder was Anne E. Bickman. Photo by Pete Miller.
Below: Heatherwood's Short Circuit, an odd eyed white American Wirehair. The owner is Anne Bickman.

Chinquapin's Happy Hooker, a black smoke female. Owner-breeder is Anne Bickman.

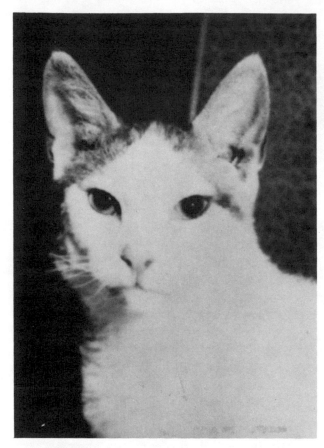

Council Rock Farm Adam of Hi-Fi. This cat was the first American Wirehair mutant. Photo courtesy of Dr. Rosemonde Peltz.

herited robust good health. It is a sweet-tempered, somewhat zany cat that adapts well to most situations and makes a quite loving house pet.

The Cat Fanciers Association, Inc. was the first to recognize this breed. The American Wirehair is bred in all colors to conform to the CFA standard.

According to the standard set for this cat the American Wirehair is a spontaneous mutation. Its coat is not only springy, dense and resilient but also coarse and hard to the touch. It is an active cat with great agility and a keen interest in its surroundings.

In proportion to the body, the head has an underlying bone structure which is round with prominent cheekbones and a well developed muzzle and chin. There is a slight whisker break. The nose in profile shows a gentle concave curve. The muzzle is well developed; the chin is firm and well developed, with no apparent malocclusion. The eyes are large, round, bright and clear. They are set well apart, and the aperture has a slight upward tilt. The body is medium to large and the back is level, with the shoulders and hips the same width. The torso is well rounded and in proportion; males will be larger than females. The legs are medium in length and bone, but well muscled and in proportion. The paws are oval and compact. The tail is in proportion to the body and tapers from the well rounded rump to a rounded tip, neither blunt nor pointed. The coat is springy, tight and medium in length. Individual hairs (including hairs within the ears) are crimped, hooked or bent. The over-all appearance of wiring and the coarseness and resilience of the coat is more important than the crimping of each hair. The density of the wired coat leads to ringlet formation rather than waves. Desirable is a coat that is very dense, resilient, crimped and coarse. Curly whiskers are also desirable.

Champion Brunsdon's Chocolate Mousse, a chocolate point Balinese female. She is owned and was bred by Rosemary J. Brunsdon. Photo by Chic Studio.

Balinese

The Balinese is a mutation. It is not a hybrid and is not a natural breed that has a history that can be traced back into antiquity, though its parent breed indeed does. In essence the Balinese is a longhaired Siamese, but it really is far more than this, and "longhaired Siamese" as a name hardly becomes this lovely breed. First, before any more information is given, it should be noted that there is no relation between the Himalayan and the Balinese. Just for quick notation: the Himalayan is a hybrid, the result of a deliberate man-made cross between Persian and a Siamese. The Balinese is an act of God, if you will. It is a mutation of longhaired kittens in an otherwise normal Siamese litter. The *type* of the cat is Siamese, but the coat is long. The Himalayan and the Balinese have nothing whatsoever in common except perhaps their color-point markings and eye color.

As stated, the first Balinese came along in a litter of normal Siamese cats with no longhairs in their background—thus it is a spontaneous mutation. It could not be called a bad Siamese coat, because a Siamese with a too-long coat has a rough and shaggy look, and such was not the case with these kittens. The Balinese coat is soft and silky; it flows. It has been described over and over in articles as "ermine-like," and it covers the entire body. To end it all, the tail is plume-like. Once breeders got over their shock at seeing these kittens in their litters, some were intelligent enough to breed to get this cat and foster this new breed. They began breeding these longhaired Siamese to others as they appeared. This increased the tendency to long hair, and I'm sure that the breeders who began this work were never sorry that they did.

It should be remembered that the initial Balinese was pure Siamese. The cat had to show three or more generations of Siamese in its background. It is a Siamese with a long coat, the type being Siamese, the coat being long. Thus, it is bred only

Balinese to Balinese or back to the Siamese for type if necessary. It is never bred to another breed and is accepted only in the four Siamese colors: seal point, blue point, lilac point and chocolate point.

Two breeders must be noted as the beginners of this breed. Mrs. Helen Smith in New York of Merry Mews Cattery showed her first longhaired Siamese at the Empire Cat Show in 1961. Since they were from Siamese CFA parents they could be shown as AOV (any other variety) entries. Even before that (in 1955) Marion Dorsey had bred a seal (point) longhair female to a blue (point) Siamese male and produced two blue (point) longhair kittens. In 1962 she wrote to Helen Smith from her Rai Mar Cattery

Champion Gaynell's Cicero, a seal point male. Breeder-owner is Nellie Sparrow. Photo by Steve's Foto.

Blue point Champion Ti-Mau's Cassandra of Virgo, owned by Patricia Horton. Breeder was Elaine K. Young.

in California; later the two women worked together to get the breed accepted. Helen Smith did not like the name Longhaired Siamese and decided to call them Balinese because of their graceful lines and the way they moved. She said they moved like Balinese dancers, with their dainty oval feet scarcely touching the ground and their plume tails waving in the air. The name and standard were submitted to the Cat Fanciers Federation and thanks to Mr. Richard Orman and Mrs. Roberta Billing CFA accepted the breed in 1963. In 1965 Rai-Mar Cattery was sold to Mrs. Sylvia Holland of Holland's Farm Cattery in California. She was a true pioneer of the Balinese, having been interested in them since 1958. Her first was Rai-Mar's Sputnik of Holland's Farm. Other breeders became interested in promoting this new breed; among them (hoping not to miss anyone) were Don and Elaine Young, Ti-Mau Cattery; Diane Murphy, El Gato Cattery; Kirsten Hovde, Chen Ye Cattery; Lieselotte Grimes, Die Lilo Cattery; Ruby Marie Greene of Verde Cattery and Mrs. Elcy

Grand Champion and Champion Gaynell's Tanisha of Die Lilo. This blue point was the second Balinese Grand Champion and the first Balinese Female Grand in the CFA. She is owned by Lieselotte A. and Frank J. Grimes. The breeder was Nellie S. Sparrow. Photo by Pete Holmes.

Crouch of E.L.C. Cattery. Acceptance of the breed continued as the cats were shown and soon the United Cat Fanciers (UCF) and the National Cat Fanciers Association (NCFA) followed, then the American Cat Association (ACA) and the American Cat Fanciers Association (ACFA), and finally in May, 1970 the CFA joined the ranks.

Today the Balinese is seen in larger numbers at shows. Their type has improved with time and crossing back to the Siamese, which is time-consuming. Grands are appearing on the scene, the first being in 1975 when a Balinese cat earned its CFA grand. This was Ti-Mau's Szabo Aki of Die Lilo, a blue point male bred by Elaine Young and owned by Lieselotte Grimes of Jacksonville, North Carolina. Breeders still accept only the four colors and wish to keep the breed pure by not crossing with another breed, thus eliminating the possibility of a cross to produce red points, torties or lynx points, which would be hybrids in the eyes of the Balinese breeder.

For those interested in this breed there is the Balinese Breeders and Fans of America International. This organization promotes unity, understanding and good fellowship among all breeders and fans of the Balinese. It is non-affiliated and non-profit. Its purpose is to promote the Balinese and to protect its bloodlines. They recognize only the four Siamese colors, and members are required

Champion Holland Farm's King Rama-Thai. This blue point male, shown in a typically curious pose, is owned by Jean Smelt. Breeder was Sylvia Holland.

Champion Gaynell's Sasha Alexi of Die Lilo. This chocolate point is owned by Lieselotte A. Grimes and was bred by Nellie S. Sparrow. Photo by Pete Holmes.

to sign and abide by a code of ethics that insures that their cats will be treated according to Pet Pride principals. No cats with any disqualifying show faults are to be used in breeding programs, and no Balinese is to be outcrossed to another breed. *Speaking Balinese*, their official newsletter (and a delightful one to read, I might add) is published every two months.

As a pet the Balinese is a happy cat, lively and very affectionate. It is easy to handle and easy to care for. They love fun and games and attention and don't care to be left alone. They are outgoing and want to be part of the family. The voice is said to be Siamese-like but softer in tone. They learn social behavior easily because of their love of people and make terrific pets. Above all, they are lovely. They carry themselves regally, gracefully and with great pride.

The Balinese is a dainty cat with tapering lines. Its head is a long tapering wedge. It is medium in size and creates a total wedge from the nose to the tips of the ears, forming a triangle with no break at the whiskers. There should be no less than the width of an eye between the eyes. The skull is flat, and there should be no bulge over the eyes and no dip in the nose. The lines are straight; the planes are flat on this cat. The nose is long and straight, a continuation of the forehead with no break, and the muzzle too is fine and wedge-shaped. The pointed ears are strikingly large; they are wide at the base, continuing the perfect lines of the wedge.

The eyes are almond-shaped and medium in size, neither protruding nor recessed, and they should never be crossed. The body of this cat is medium in size, dainty, long and svelte. The cat has fine bone but it is well muscled. The body is tubular, and sleek lines continue down the body with a tight abdomen—no bulging and no sagging. The neck is long and slender. The legs are long and slim, with hind legs higher than the front; the feet are dainty, small and oval. The tail is long and thin, tapering to a fine point with tail hair that spreads like a plume. The coat is basically long, fine and silky without a downy undercoat.

The Balinese is accepted in the blue point, the chocolate point, the seal point and the lilac point.

Arbayi Dominic, a seal point Birman kitten. He is owned and was bred by Mrs. Jean Park of England. Photo by Neville Chadwick.

Birman

The Birman is believed to have originated in the Temple of Lao-Tsun in the ancient land of Burma. All information leads to the fact that this is a natural breed of Burma rather than a product of breeding, since no records exist concerning a breeding program that would have produced it. To understand the breed's background, you must know the legend about the cat. There are varying legends, but they all have the same basic story; the one reported here seems to be the one most repeated and was sent to me by an early pioneer with this breed. The story goes that the Birman, or the Sacred Cat of Burma as it was known, was to be found centuries ago in beautiful temples built by the Khmer people of Asia in order to pay homage to their gods. These temples housed pure white cats, and it was believed that after death the priests returned to the temple in the form of these cats. One temple, that of Lao-Tsun, housed a beautiful golden goddess with sapphire-blue eyes who watched over this transmigration of souls. Mun-Ha, one of the most beloved priests, whose beard had been braided by the great god Son-Hio, often knelt in meditation before the golden goddess Tsun-Kyan-Kse. Sinh, a beautiful and faithful white temple cat, was always by his side. One night as the moon rose the temple was attacked, and Mun-Ha was killed. At the moment of Mun-Ha's death, Sinh placed his feet upon his fallen master and faced the golden goddess. The white hairs of his body were as golden as the light radiated from the golden goddess, her beautiful blue eyes became his very own, and his four white legs shaded downwards to a velvety brown—but where his feet rested on his dead master the white remained, denoting purity. The next morning, all the temple cats had this distinctive look. Seven days after the priest died the cat died too, carrying the priest's soul into heaven. These cats became even more sacred to the Buddhists.

Grand Champion Rindy's Haven Yomanda, the first female Grand Champion Birman. This seal point is owned and was bred by Ed and Harriet Rindfleisch. Photo by Steve's Foto.

Then a time came when the Brahmins felt that the Kittahs (priests) were practicing a false religion, so they raided the temple. A number of Europeans, among them August Pavie and Major Russell-Gordon, were able to help the Kittahs move across the mountains of Burma into Tibet, taking with them their cats. A new Temple of Lao-Tsun was built underground; photos circulated today express the serene chosen area situated to the east of Lake Incaougji, between Magaoug and Sembo. The Kittahs still lived in that spot as late as 1898.

As a gift to the French who had helped them, the Burmese people sent a pair of sacred cats from the temple in 1919. The male had died on the way to Nice, France, but the female (named Sita) was pregnant. Sita gave birth to a perfectly marked female, Poupee. From 1926 through 1935 many articles were published about this breed. Marcel Reney in his book calls attention to the sacred cats' transition to France, pointing out that they were smuggled out by an unfaithful attendant in charge of the temple. Whatever the controversy, that they arrived in France and that the breed survived to become recognized by French breeders must be looked upon as the important facts. Rightfully, the Birmans are now considered a French breed, since French breeders had strived to preserve the race and had established several known catteries in France. In France, the breed is known as the *Sacre de Birmanie;* each country has its own term. Nonetheless, when spoken of as the "Sacred Cat of Burma," the race is set apart with great merit owing to its own charm.

During the early years of perfecting the breed, in Berlin, Germany, Frau Hanna Krueger was establishing and perpetuating to the fourth generation of German registration the foundation stock of a German line. Records speak of Fandango, a noted sire that was given the title of "father of today's Birmans." It was after the death of Frau Krueger that a known French breeder, Mlle. Gillet, acquired the little flock and herded it back to France. The early pedigrees trace the lineages as they fuse, branching out with exports to many countries.

Mlle. Marcelle Adam, owner of the Madalpour Cattery, was an avid breeder and supporter of the race and one of the first to work with the Birman in France. She was the President of Federation Feline Francaise (FFF), the organization that composed the original standard for this cat. All countries in which the Birman is recognized adopted the standard, which remains basically as it originally was except for a few minor changes made in 1973. In France a specialty organization called the Cercle Du Chat Sacre de Birmanie furthers the interest in the breed. Two of the first catteries noted on early pedigrees are Madalpour, the prefix of Mlle. Adam, and KaaBaa, associated with a Miss Boyer.

Dr. and Mrs. John H. Seipel of Fairfax, Virginia were the first breeders to import the Sacre de Birmanie into the United States from France. Irrouaddi Du Clos Fleuri, known as "Waddi," was the first Birman import to the Seipels. A male arriving in 1959 was considered to be a chocolate point. Later came Josika Du Clos

Above: Rindy's Haven Yanzi, a seal point, owned by Janice Borgne. Breeders were Harriet and Ed Rindfleisch.
Below: Champion Solomon von Assindia of Smokeyhill, a seal point, owned by Elizabeth Brown of England. The breeder was Frau A. Hackmann of Germany. Photo by Anne Cumbers.

Fleuri, a blue point female known as "Josie." A few months later Joanne d'Ormailley, a seal point female known as "Mitty," arrived. In 1961, Kairos de Lugh, a seal point from the well known cattery of Madame Yvonne Drossier, Paris, France took up residence with the Seipel family.

In Battombak, Cambodia, Mr. Carter Townes and his houseboy, ImDim, owned two lovely cats from Tibet. Mlle. Gillet, a well-known breeder of the race in France, was associated with the bloodlines of the two cats, Schaiffia of Asia and Boke Khmer. Mr. Townes had visited his sister in Tacoma, Washington bringing with him the two cats. Three kittens were born from this pair of cats during Mr. Townes' stay, and Mrs. Gertrude Griswold acquired two of them—Pkaa, and a male, Klaa Khmer. A tie-in was established and in 1963 a noted French breeder, Madame Simone Poirier, agreed to send Mrs. Griswold a male, known in the U.S. as Korrigan of Clover Creek, and a female, Leslie de la Regnardarie. A short time later Madame Anne Marie Moulin exported Opale de Khlaramour. These five cats established Mrs. Griswold's American stock of Birmans. Korrigan of Clover Creek, like Hamlet de Madalpour, seems to be on most of the old pedigrees. Although now retired from breeding, Korrigan is residing with a Mr. and Mrs. Moore in Maryland and was seventeen years old at the time of this writing.

Col. and Mrs. Martin H. Rau of Lao-Tsun Cattery were stationed in France with the American government. They first saw the Birman in France in 1961, and when orders for their return to the U.S. arrived in 1964 five Birmans came home with them: International Champion Karyne d'Ormailley, purchased in France from Madame Vandaille, her breeder; Mousmee du Clos Fleuri, Mirtus du Clos Fleuri and Mikado du Clos Fleuri, bred by Madame Surcel; and Neko do Lao-Tusn, a tot from Karyne and Hamlet of Madalpour. Neko can be found on many pedigrees, and all the Grand Champions in the United States have his lineage.

Around the same time English fanciers were doing their own scouting with thoughts of establishing the breed in England. Mrs. Elsie Fisher visited a show in Paris in 1965 and, with her partner, Mrs. H. Richard, imported Nouky de Mon Reve and Orlamonde de Khlaramour. Osaka de Lugh and Pipo du Clos Fleuri soon

Smokeyhill Nhan Leequeon, a blue point. Owner-breeder is Elizabeth Brown. Photo by Anne Cumbers.

followed. Two German males also were imported into England: Ghandi von Assindia, a blue point, went to Mrs. Fisher of the Praha Cattery, and Solomon von Assindia, a seal point, went to Elizabeth Brown of Smokeyhill Cattery. They both came from the cattery of Frau A. Hackmann. England accepted the Birman to championship status in 1966.

In the United States, a noted Persian breeder, Miss Verner Clum, acquired Birmans from Col. and Mrs. Rau. First came Neko and Opom, then Opaz and Pia. Miss Clum showed them extensively, and a memorable day in Birman history came during the first championship showing at Madison Square Garden in 1967 (prior to this CFA had allowed the Primary Record registrations). Neko de Lao-Tsun of Gaylands and Pia de Lao-Tsun of Gaylands made newspaper headlines. Miss Clum retired from breeding, and the Birmans were adopted by Mr. and Mrs. Ralph Griswold. They were Neko, Pia, Opom de Lao-Tsun of Gaylands and Opaz de Lao-Tsun of Gaylands, and a seal point male bred by Miss Clum, Gayland's Quiff of Griswold. The lines continued, crossing with the early imports of the Griswold Cattery. Shortly after Mrs. Griswold launched her program with the Birman, Mrs. Mildred Whitehead became the third American breeder when she imported Ch. Primrose du Clos Fleuri, a fine seal point female.

The Cat Fanciers Association has recorded the following grand champion Birmans to date: Griswold's Romar of Bybee, a blue point owned by Mrs. Grayson; Keystone Victor of Jazze, owned by Mr. and Mrs. Johnson; and Tai Ming's Verner of Jandra, Tai Ming's Xaruff of Jandra and Rindey's Haven Danny, all three owned by Jim and Pam Pugliano. The first two female Grand Champions are Rindy's Haven Yomanda and Rindy's Haven X-Terri, both blue points owned by Ed and Harriet Rindfleisch. Other known grands are Grand Premier Duvall's Tam-I-Koo, owned by Ms. Marie Trujillo, and Reaycrest Mythe Neko of Pee-Wee, co-owned by Darlene Plourd and Geraldine Ledoyen of Canada.

Birmans are true individuals to own, adjusting well to family liv-

Hephzibah Caeruleus of Mask Rider, a blue point male, owned by Joe and Fay Mosier. Breeder was Margaret John of England. Photo by Angela Sayer.

International Champion Smokeyhill Kwan Yin, owned by Ed and Harriet Rindfleisch. Breeder was R.E. Brown of England.

ing. They are noted for their dispositions and charm of personality. They do not upset easily if left out of things, but to cage a Birman breaks its spirit. They are delightful companions, adjusting and mixing well with other animals in the house, and they are intelligent and easy to train. They also breed well with few problems.

One distinctive feature of this breed deserves particular mention: the white paws, or gloves, such as no other breed possess. The feature is believed to be caused by a white spotting gene and represents a low grade of piebald spotting. In addition to this feature the old Birman in France was known to have the golden halo, which was a faint touch of gold over the entire back of the cat, making it look as though a mist of gold had settled over the outer coat of the cat's back. This is passed down through generations and can be found most markedly in pure bloodlines.

The white paws, or gloves, of the cat should be full at the wrist or ankle joint, symmetrical, and pure white. All four paws should be evenly matched, the cut-off at the third joint, an even line across the paw. The back paws are covered with the same white and end in a point called the "laces" that goes up the back of the leg.

The Birman has a strong, broad and rounded head. The slightly convex forehead slopes back, and there is a flat spot just in front of the ears. Its nose is Roman in shape, with nostrils set low on the nose leather. Its cheeks are full, and the jaw is heavy. Ears are set to the side as much as to the top of the head; eyes are slightly round. The body is long but stocky, carried low over the legs, which should be medium in length and heavy-boned. The paws are firm and very large, with toes bound closely together. The silken coat is long, curly on the stomach, and the ruff usually is outstanding in thick heavy fur. The fur never mats or tangles and requires much less grooming than the coat of other longhairs. The tail is rather long, presenting an odd shape when the cat displays it as a plume.

The Birman is accepted in four colors. The original was the seal point; the blue point came into being in the early 1960's, and the lilac and chocolate points came later.

Champion Kejo Kyrie, the first Bombay Champion in the CFA. Owner-breeder is Pat Taylor.

Kejo Cutty Sark of Burmaden, a male Bombay, owned by Evelyn Piriano. Breeder was Pat Taylor.

Bombay

These cats were originated by Nikki Horner of Shawnee Cattery. They are a man-made hybrid breed, not a natural breed or unplanned mutation. Two already established breeds were crossed to produce the Bombay. Bombays have been referred to, because of their looks, as the "patent leather kids with the new-penny eyes"—and it's easy to see why when one has seen these beautiful cats or a picture of them. The black fur seems to shine, and the eyes are a new-penny copper against a jet black coat. They were named, it seems, for the black leopard of India and are referred to also as "mini panthers."

The two original breeds used to produce the Bombay were a black American Shorthair (Gr. Ch. Shawnee Anthracite) and a Burmese (Gr. Ch. Hill House Daniella). Only the best of the two breeds was used, and the Bombay combines the black color and hardy type of the black American Shorthair and the sleek coat of the Burmese. The Bombay was accepted by CFA for championship status on May 1, 1976. Kejo Kyrie is the first Bombay champion on record. In Canada, Evelyn Piriano brought the first Bombay into the country in 1975, purchased from Pat Taylor's Kejo Cattery. Now there are Bombays in Kentucky, Canada, Arizona, Illinois, Pennsylvania and Texas.

Breeding Bombays is easy, as they breed true. Bombay to Bombay will produce all Bombays. It is not necessary to breed to either Burmese or American Shorthair unless there is a shortage of fresh lines, and in this case any offspring of Burmese and black American Shorthair may be registered as Bombays. At this time, therefore, matings of Bombay to Burmese, Bombay to Bombay or Bombay to black American Shorthair all produce offspring registrable as Bombays. Black is dominant, and black kittens result on the first cross. Type and coat texture, plus eye color, are controlled by good breeding practices.

Shawnee Mozambique of Kejo, owned by Pat Taylor. Breeder was Nikki Horner.

According to Mrs. Piriano, the Bombay is a beautiful cat to own. I agree that it is a striking animal. The color and sheen of the coat immediately capture attention and the copper eyes set against the black fur make for a beautiful contrast. According to their owners, Bombays are delightful to own as well as decorative. They have an even temperament and are quite playful, although not too talkative. Actually, given the Burmese and the American Short-hair temperaments, their personality should be ideal. They get along well with other cats and are very hale and hearty. They grow rapidly when young and mature earlier than some other breeds. They are affectionate and like to be close to their owner. They don't like to be ignored and resort to all kinds of antics to get attention. They are constant purrers. The males are clumsy despite their graceful look, but the females are very graceful. Maybe this is just typical of overzealous males. It is my belief that this breed, when seen by more of the fancy, will become quite popular. It is a lovely addition to the cat fancy and striking to say the least.

The head of the Bombay should be pleasantly round, without flat planes. The face should be full and there should be considerable breadth between the eyes. The cat has a short, well-developed muzzle, and there should be a visible nose break. Its ears are medium in size, broad at the base with slightly rounded tips, and set well apart on a rounded skull tilting slightly forward. The eyes are round and set wide apart. The body is medium, muscular and neither cobby nor rangy. The tail is straight and medium in length. The coat has a fine, short, satin-like texture; it should be very close-lying, with a shimmering patent leather sheen. The mature Bombay should be black to the roots, with black nose leather and paw pads, and the cat's eye color should range from yellow to deep copper. The copper is more desirable than the yellow—the greater the depth, brilliance and intensity of the copper color the better.

Grand Champion and Quad. Champion Bili Bash's Azure of K-La, a blue British Shorthair, owned by Ed and Kathy Rohrer. Breeders were Al and Alice Dickens. Photo by Larry Levy.

British Shorthair

The British Shorthair is the English equivalent of the American Shorthair. It appears from records that it was first shown in England in the late 1800's. However, World War I brought the fancy to a stop and affected the British Shorthair as it was known. Stocks were small, so breeders had trouble getting enough cats reflecting the British Shorthair standard to work with. It was necessary for the English to use the Persian in their shorthairs to regain the standard they desired. However, the GCCF was strict in its registration; because the British Shorthair was an established breed, the GCCF ruled that such crosses did not produce cats that met registration qualifications. Therefore a supplementary register was used, and cats produced from Persian and British Shorthair crosses were registered in this supplementary register until three generations of British Shorthair to British Shorthair had again purified the breed. Then the cat gained acceptance into the regular register.

By introducing Persian blood, the English were able to produce the cat we see today. It has a hint of Persian, but it is distinctively British and unlike our American Shorthair in type. It was what the English had always believed their British Shorthairs to be and what Americans have adopted and begun to breed and show with great pride. It is no wonder, as it is a lovely animal. By the 1950's in England the British Shorthair again appeared on the show scene.

American stock comes from the top catteries in England. The breed has been accepted in bits and pieces, so to speak, in that the British Blue was seen as a separate breed in some associations at first, but now more and more associations are recognizing this breed in all its natural colors. ACFA was the first to accept them at all, accepting only the blues and blacks. CCA and CFF recognized

Champion Jindivik Romany Boy of Overland (Imp), owned by Betti-Jane Myjak. Breeder was Mrs. Iris Burgess.

only the British Blue. ACFA was then the first to accept all the colors, followed by CCA in May, 1976; other associations later followed. CFA has now recognized them for registration with a tentative standard. All associations have the same standard—the same as the English. In the United States, as in England, British Shorthairs are bred only to other British Shorthairs and not back to the Persian.

The British Shorthair is charming and loving to both people and to other animals. It is very smart and gentle. These cats are not easily upset; they are active and take an interest in everything around them. They can be quiet and loving, aloof and also amusing and playful at times. They can be left alone to entertain themselves but are glad to have your company. Basically, they are sound, healthy cats that survive well and breed well due to their natural build. There has been little interference in the structure of the breed, so the British Shorthair has the attributes of a natural breed, with its instincts intact and its body sound.

To distinguish this breed from the American Shorthair, simply put them side by side. The touch of the Persian is in the British Shorthair, making it and the American Shorthair different in coat texture and in type. The British Shorthair has a broad head with well-rounded contours when viewed from any angle. The cheeks are well developed, the nose is short and broad with a good muzzle. The ears are set far enough apart that the base of the inner ear is perpendicular to the outer corner of the eye; they are medium in size, broad at the base and rounded at the tips. The neck is short and bull-like, particularly in the male. The eyes are round, large, well opened and set to show breadth of the nose. The body is

Two British Shorthair kittens in an inquisitive pose. Photo by Lydia Messier.

medium to large, with broad and flat shoulders. The hips are the same width as the shoulders. The chest is broad and rounded. The body is well-knit and powerful. The legs are strong, the feet and toes well rounded. The tail is in proportion to the body and thick at the base, with a slight taper. The coat is short, well-bodied, resilient and firm to the touch. It is not woolly and not double-coated, but it is dense.

The British Shorthair is accepted in the following colors: copper-eyed white, the odd-eyed white and the blue-eyed white; chinchilla silver and shaded silver; black smoke and the blue smoke; tortoiseshell and tortoiseshell and white; the blue-cream, the bi-color and the parti-color, plus the tabby pattern in spotted, classic and mackerel in the following colors: blue, brown, cream, red and silver.

Overleaf:

Shamba Letu Meiko of Grenouille Mi-Ke, a calico Japanese Bobtail female, owned by Mr. and Mrs. Gil Belanger and bred by Carolyn McLaughlin.

Overleaf:

Above: *Left to right, Grand Champion Tsar Blu's Chip o'Willy, Grand Champion Tsar Blu's Flash of Sereshka, Champion Tsar Blu's Moorka and Champion Tsar Blu's Silver Sonnet, a Russian Blue litter bred by Donna Fuller.*

Below: *Grand Champion Velva's Cobalt Baron of Tsar Blu, a Russian Blue male, owned by Donna Fuller and bred by Diana Doernberg. Photos by Heritage Studio.*

Overleaf:

Above: *June B. Mourao's Double Champion, a blue point Himalayan male, Royal Row's Prince Match-abelli. He was bred by Georgia Rowe.*

Below: *Sue McKenney's white Persian, Samar Meeja of Sue Mc, a Grand and Triple Champion. Photos by Bud Bidwell and Pet Portraits.*

Overleaf:

Grand Champion Jindivik Apollo of Overland, a cream mackerel tabby British Shorthair, owned by Bettijane Myjak and bred by Mrs. Iris Burgess. Photo by Larry Levy.

Overleaf:

CFA Grand Champion Ti-Mau's Szabo Aki of Die Lili, a blue point Balinese male, owned by Lieselotte A. Grimes. Photo by Larry Levy.

Overleaf:

Above: *Virginia Lane's Triple Champion, Purring Lane Sweet Fire, a flame point Himalayan female.*

Below: *A basketful of Ragdoll kittens; photo through the courtesy of Ann Baker.*

Overleaf:

Above, left: *Kejo Cutty Sark of Burmaden, a male Bombay owned by Evelyn Piriano and bred by Pat Taylor.*

Above, right: *Double Grand Champion and Quadruple Champion Crescent Dantara of Amadear, a ruddy Abyssinian female owned by Dr. and Mrs. Duane E. Young, and bred by Dr. Henrietta N. Shirk.*

Below, left: *Shawnee Bata Hari of Kejo, a female Bombay owned by Pat Taylor and bred by Nikki Horner.*

Below, right: *Double Champion Da-Glo's Loreal, a seal tortie point Colorpoint Shorthair female from Da-Glo Cattery, Virginia.*

Overleaf:

A black smoke American Wirehair with the characteristic golden eyes.

Overleaf:

Anthony Morace's Double Champion Mor-Ace's Hephzibah, a bronze Egyptian Mau female. Photo by Kevin T. Sullivan.

Overleaf:

Above, left: *Champion Cidar-O's Puff n' Stuff, a blue cream female Persian owned and bred by Mr. and Mrs. Steve Davis. Photo by Chet Burak.*

Above, right: *A blue British Shorthair, Trafalgar's Indigo of K-La, owned by Mr. and Mrs. Rohrer and bred by Joel Presser. Photo by Tom Young.*

Below, left: *Double Champion Gallantree's Uncas, a ruddy male Abyssinian owned and bred by Mr. and Mrs. Ron Bauer. Photo by Jensen.*

Below, right: *A blue point Himalayan male, Misty-Mount's Balin, a Triple Champion, owned and bred by Mr. and Mrs. Skip Vincelett. Photo by Chet Burak.*

Overleaf:

Above, left: *Lydia Messier's blue British Shorthair, Broadneir Happy Talk of Tintagalon, a Grand and International Champion.*

Above, right: *Champion An Je Bar's Shady Lady, a classic tabby Exotic Shorthair, owned and bred by Joan Stayton. Photo by Darise.*

Below: *Double Champion R.M. Rise of Thornton's Desert, white male Turkish Angora, owned by Mrs. George Thornton and bred by Mr. and Mrs. Roy Porter.*

Overleaf:

A ruddy Somali male, Champion L'Air De Rauch Rocky Raccoon of Foxtail, owned by Patricia Nell Warren and bred by Mrs. M. Rauch. Photo by Manny Greenhaus.

Overleaf:

Weasel, a natural mink male Tonkinese, owned by Trigger Alpert.

Overleaf:

Above: *Grand and Quadruple Champion Trafalgar's Sativa of Overland, a blue British Short-hair, owned by Bettijane Myjak and bred by Mr. and Mrs. Joel Presser.*

Below: *Sreyasi, a honey mink female Tonkinese, and friend, owned by Mr. and Mrs. Morgan Morrison. Photo by Morgan Morrison.*

Overleaf:

Above: *Barbara Distinti's Double Grand Champion and Quadruple Champion, Maluce's Mokey Joe of Ky-Ro, a black Persian male.*

Below: *Champion Torio Jumping Jack, an amber eyed white Turkish Angora, owned and bred by Mr. and Mrs. Thomas Torio. Both photos by Larry Levy.*

Premier Grand Champion Tintagalon Churchill, a British Short-hair, owned by John Warden. Breeder was Lydia Messier.

Double Grand Champion Shawnee Hail A Star of Mandalay, a sable Burmese female, owned by Herbert Zwecker. Breeder was Nikki Horner. Photo by Larry Levy.

Burmese

The history of the Burmese begins with one cat that was brought forth from the Orient to this country by Dr. Joseph Thompson in 1930. This cat was a brown or walnut colored female called Wong Mau. It is believed that this cat and others like it were part of the Asiatic group of cats that includes the Siamese and Korat. These cats were found in Siam and Burma in early times, and a solid brown or self brown cat is known to have existed in these countries and to have some relation to the Korat and Siamese. Dr. Clyde Keeler worked with this breed in this country, as did Dr. Thompson and his geneticist assistant Billie Gerst. However, the offspring from Wong Mau's breedings with Siamese here were thought to be simply poor Siamese. Since there was only one Burmese to begin with, she was bred in 1932 to what was then considered even by Siamese breeders to be a fine example of a Siamese, a cat named Tai Mau. This mating produced a cat called Topaz Mau and many more offspring which led to the Burmese we see today. It was discovered that the offspring of a litter between a Siamese and a Burmese resulted in a kitten, light in color somewhere between the color of the Siamese and Burmese. It was later determined that breeding back one of these intermediate-colored kittens to others of the same color or to the original mother (who was believed to be carrying the necessary brown gene) could produce kittens with the proper dark brown color that was truly Burmese. These dark brown Burmese bred true; to maintain good type, breeding back to the Siamese was not recommended.

Soon interest grew in the breed, and more cats came onto the scene. It is important to note that although both the Siamese and Burmese are Asiatic in background, the type of the Burmese is not the Oriental type of the Siamese. American breeders strive to maintain the proper Burmese type and beautiful coloring. They

Above: Quadruple Grand Champion and Gr. Ch. Chinthe's Microbe, a sable male. Breeder-owner is Mary DePew. Photo by Creative Photographers.
Opposite, above: Champion Shawnee Cinnamon Stop of Walnut, owned by Suzanne Beedy. Breeder was Nikki Horner. Photo by Sonneman.
Opposite, below: Double Grand Champion Koni Kai's Niki, owned by Carolyn L. Osier. Breeders were Mr. and Mrs. Clarence Hall. Photo by Jim Cooper.

consider the Burmese to be in a way, an American breed because it was perfected here and promoted here. The breed is also known in England, but from what I have seen of English Burmese, their Burmese reflects a more Oriental look. Our Burmese is not Siamese in type or bone structure. By 1934 American breeders were looking for the Burmese to be recognized, and in 1936 the breed was accepted for registration. In 1947 CFA withdrew this privilege because of breeding practices, but renewed it in 1957.

America's first all American Burmese was owned by Mrs. Hoag of Bridle Trail; called Sherwood's Tria, it was from the cattery of Florence Kanoffee. Mr. and Mrs. Albert Slaughter's cat Kokomo became the first American grand champion.

In addition to the sable Burmese we also see some fine champagne Burmese at shows. Champagne Burmese first appeared in litters of sable Burmese, and it was decided that the same theory applied here as applies to the chocolate point Siamese. The champagne Burmese carries a gene for diluting the pigmentation of the sable Burmese. For a champagne cat to be born, the gene for this dilution must be present in both parents. The champagne Burmese is a golden beige; there is a slight shading on the face and ears, but these are not "points," as in a Siamese. In fact, the sable Burmese has the same markings—they just don't show up as much on the darker color.

Quint. Grand Champion Shawnee Route 66 of Mandalay. This sable male is owned by Herbert Zwecker and was bred by Nikki Horner. Photo by Dudley Ashwood.

Grand Champion Motet's Troubador of Senshu, a sable male, owned by Vern and Cheryl Maddox. Breeder was Carol Sebesta.

As a writer and researcher I have had contact with owners of many different breeds, and those who own the "Burm" are only too happy to tell about their breed. I can believe that what I hear is true, as my husband and I have had occasion to handle the Burm, and it is a delight that is hard to explain. There is just something about the breed. They are very affectionate to begin with. They also tend to love perpetual motion. They love people and being loved and being cuddled. This is a cat you can touch and hold. Burmese are a joy to own, we are told, as they are sweet. They have sweet voices and nice manners, and they can be very dignified.

They can be warmly affectionate or active bundles of energy. They do not like being alone and are very social. They also can be jealous. I have been told that they understand the moods of their owners and tend to reflect them. They also are supposed to have a strong cat family unit, with the male as attentive to babies as the female is. Burms can get angry—and when they do, watch out. The Burmese is a brown bundle of love that begs you to take it home, and I have found that men are particularly attracted to this cat.

The Burmese cat is not a fragile shorthair. It is a medium-sized cat with good bone structure, good muscular development, expressive eyes and a sweet face. Its head is pleasingly round without

Grand Champion Burma Road's Detour of Senshu. This sable male was bred by Bev Stevens and is owned by Vern and Cheryl Maddox.

flat planes. The face is full, with breadth between the eyes, tapering slightly to a short, well developed muzzle. There is a visible nose break. The ears are medium in size, alert, tilting slightly forward, broad at the base with slightly rounded tips, and set well apart on a rounded skull. The eyes are set far apart and are of good round shape. The body is medium in size, muscular and compact. The Burmese has an ample rounded chest and a level back from shoulder to tail. The tail is straight and medium in length; the coat is a fine, glossy, satin-like texture that is short and close-lying. The color of the sable is a rich, warm sable brown shading imperceptibly to a slightly lighter hue on the underparts, but otherwise without markings or shadings of any kind. The nose leather and paw pads are brown, and the eye color is gold—the more depth and brilliance the better. The champagne Burmese is a warm beige, shading to a pale gold-tan underside; a gradual shading in older cats is to be allowed. Pads and nose leather are a light warm brown. Some associations even accept a blue and a platinum Burmese.

Tok-Lat's Fudge Bar of Tatha-Gata, a sable female, owned by Esther Epstein. Breeder was Joan Batchelor. Photo by Buckingham.

Grand Champion Arista Muffet of Bo-Wood, a female Chartreux, owned by Mr. and Mrs. B.L. Wood. Breeder was Mrs. Gen Scudder. Photo by Brian Allen.

Chartreux

The Chartreux is believed to be a natural breed, one that originated in France and has been a part of the French countryside and French towns for centuries. Breeders of this cat take great exception to its being lumped with other breeds or being called man-made or being misidentified. The last-named case occurs most often with other solid-colored shorthaired cats, but the Chartreux is a breed unto itself. They are totally natural and totally French.

M. Jean Simonnet traced the background of this cat and was referred to the 1723 edition of the *Universal Dictionary of Commerce, of Natural History and of the Arts and Trades* which contained the interesting fact that the Chartreux was a common name given to a sort of cat which had fur tending toward blue in color. Chartreux in this dictionary also referred to a "Pile de Chartreux," which was a kind of wool imported from Spain and used in the making of the finest woolens. However, as early as 1558 a poet, du Bellay, wrote about his cat and noted that it was not entirely gray, as the cats are in France. It seems as though the general feeling was that France indeed was known for gray cats which roamed freely. These blue cats were actually gray or slate-colored.

Legends exist about the name Chartreux. Some believe that the name came from the religious order of the Carthusian monks. These monks were supposed to have brought the cat from the Cape of Good Hope in the 17th century to their mother house, "Le Grand Chartreux." The cats lived with the monks, and thus some say that the monks named them after their order. The cats may well have lived with the monks, as they did with many other groups and individuals, but there is no evidence that the monks named them. The name could just as well have come from the above mentioned "Pile de Chartreux." This would have been a

Bo-Wood's Twinkle, owned and bred by Mr. and Mrs. B.L. Wood.
Photo by Brian Allen.

good choice of name for a cat with a woolly coat. There is no way
to be certain how the cat got its name. However, there is evidence
that a cat called Chartreux was known from early times.

In 1748 Diderot referred to this cat in his *Les Bijoux Indiscrets*.
The French naturalist Buffon showed great interest in the cat as
early as 1756. In his *Natural History* he related that there were
four common cats in Europe: the domestic, the Spanish (believed
to be a tortie), the Angora and the Chartreux. Others, including
Linne and also Rene Primevere Lesson in his *Manuel Mammaogie*
published in 1827, agreed on these four varieties. In 1775, Buffon,
in his *Natural History,* described the blue Persian by saying it has
a coat like the Angora and the color of the Chartreux, thereby
referring to the Chartreux by its known name and color. It is
believed that also in this book is a picture in black and white showing a cat identified as the Chartreux sitting on a rooftop, thus
denoting it as a domestic cat that roamed the streets of France. It
has been described as a cat with a straight nose, a domestic cat

with no break or stop in the nose, with longer hair than the domestic cat, a woolly textured coat and a tail that is carried straight out and pointed at the neck. In a later edition of this work the cat is shown in a color photo, and it is said that it was slate gray with blackish brown at the base and heavy coat. The coloring was a clear, solid gray, without striping, barring, spotting or any other markings.

In France, breeding began about 1928. The first cats appeared at a show under the name Chartreux in 1931 in Paris and were shown by a Mlle. Leger, who had moved around 1928 to Belle-Ile, an island off the northwestern tip of France. She found a large number of blue cats with short fur at Le Palais, the main city of Belle-Ile. In the country all these cats were the same type despite

Three Chartreux kittens: Gamonal Luciole, Gamonal Lutteur and Gamonal Luron. All three are owned and were bred by Helen Gamon. Photo by Portrait World.

Champion Vandale de St. Pierre, owned by Helen Gamon. Breeder was Madame S. Bastide. Photo by Portrait World.

breeding with other European cats. She acquired the cats and bred a blue male, Coquito, to a blue female, Marquire. All the kittens were blue and perfectly typed. One offspring, named Mignonne, went on to win an international championship, the Belgian Challenge Cup and the Prize of Esthetics in Paris in 1933.

After WWII the registry of purebreds in France was a mess, and there were few Chartreux left. British Shorthairs and other blue cats were roaming across Europe. To restore the Chartreux, some breeders tried Persian breeding and lost type; some tried the British Blue, but it was not the same. Finally it was decided to use as foundation stock only those French blue cats found in the countryside that met the standard.

In the United States Helen Gamon was one of several people who imported the Chartreux and sought to get it recognized. She began her work in 1970. Three of the original ten imports were from the cattery of Mlle. Leger, de Guerveur cattery. An effort had been made and continued to be made to breed out everything but Chartreux in pedigrees until they were pure again. They have now been accepted by ACFA, UCF, NCFA, CROWN, CCA and are in the process of being accepted by CFF. ACA first accepted them and then withdrew recognition, wanting them registered as

British, which breeders claim they are not. CFA wants them as Exotics, which again they are not. They are a natural breed with a natural history. They breed true, and all pedigrees being used today in this country reflect pure Chartreux breeding.

According to Mrs. Gamon, who has been a tremendous help with this breed, the breed is energetic and playful but of a very placid temperament for a cat. The voice is mostly quiet and seldom heard. Chartruex prefer dogs to cats and act more like dogs

Bo-Wood's Liette, a Chartreux kitten, owned and bred by Mr. and Mrs B.L. Wood.

An excellent representative of the Chartreux breed, Ch. Taquin de St. Pierre is owned by Helen Gamon and was bred by Madame S. Bastide. This portrait can also be found in color on page 164.

than cats. They exercise in spurts, galloping around for a short period and that is it for the day. They are not destructive, being calm and sweet and very affectionate. They behave well and discipline easily. They are not timid and may defend their owners. Any sound from them is often a chirp rather than a meow, and their purr is a deep loud buzzing.

The Chartreux has a large and broad head, but not a round head. The nose is short and straight, with a slight stop allowed. The muzzle is narrow in relation to the head, but it is not pointed. The cheeks are well developed; the neck is short, strong and heavy-set, and the jaws are powerful. The cat has a sweet, smiling expression. The ears are small to medium, with slightly rounded tips and set high on the head. Inside furnishings cover one-half of the ear. There is an extremely fine coat on the outer ear. The eyes are large, round and very expressive. The color can be pale gold to orange. The body is large, well proportioned and robust, with large, muscular shoulders and a well developed chest. The over-all appearance is of a solid and muscular cat. Breeders particularly emphasize the difference in size between the male and female. The male is much more massive. The tail is heavier at the base, tapering slightly to the tip. The coat texture is dense and soft, with silver highlights. The texture and length are longer and less flat than that of the Domestic Shorthair, and the female's coat may be silkier and thinner than the male's. The color is any shade of gray-blue with silver-gray nose leather and foot pads that are rose-taupe.

Colorpoint Shorthair

A background on the Colorpoint Shorthair would have to incorporate the histories of the breeds that went into its making, since this cat began as a hybrid, the result of crossing two separate breeds. Today, different breeders view the cat differently. Some say it is a Siamese cat of a different color, some say it is a separate breed altogether. Most countries and cat associations place the Colorpoint Shorthair within the Siamese class, except the major US association, and it does not. Those who feel strongly that the Colorpoint is not a Siamese stand firm in their beliefs. While much has been written both pro and con on the matter, for our purposes we will consider it a separate breed.

In type the Colorpoint Shorthair is a Siamese in every way. However, to achieve the colors of red, tortie (in all its varieties) and lynx (in all its varieties), it was necessary to cross the Siamese with another breed. The American Shorthair provided the colors necessary and so the usual cross was between a red Domestic and a seal point Siamese. The first cross produced solid colored cats because the Domestic did not carry the recessive gene for color points necessary in both parents for offspring to be colorpointed. Thus a cross back to a Siamese was necessary to produce the first generation of Colorpoint Shorthairs which usually included solid color cats as well as colorpoint ones. Going back to the Domestic Shorthair after color has been established is not necessary and harms the type which is supposed to be the extreme Siamese type. If outcrosses are made again they are made back to the Siamese for type, with fewer colorpoint colors, but more type resulting.

Opposite:
Champion J-Bar's Bob Kat of JoRene, a seal lynx point Colorpoint Shorthair. He is owned by Dr. Irene B. Horowitz. Breeders were Jack and Barbara Collins.

Patapaw Running Deer, a chocolate cream point female. Breeder-owner is Marilyn T. Buchanan. Photo by Ben Craven.

The typical Colorpoint Shorthair kitten is born white as with other pointed cats; the skin begins to pick up a reddish color when it is about a week old if it is to be a red point. Otherwise there may be vague point markings, and the paw pads may show a speckled appearance usually denoting a tortie point.

Creating a lynx point took a little more effort for perfection in the markings. The cross was between a Siamese and a mackerel tabby Domestic which produced hybrids that looked like Domestic mackerel tabbies but carried the colorpoint gene. Bred back to the Siamese a lynx point could result.

As more and more Colorpoint Shorthairs become grands within a distinct breed, and grands as a color within the Siamese class, the effort that went into developing this cat will be well rewarded. Technically, the cat will always be a hybrid—a cross between two breeds. However, as with most hybrids, a new look has not developed. The Colorpoint Shorthair still looks like a Siamese except for color, thus the reason for their being regarded as a Siamese in some countries and associations. Other hybrid breeds that have been created have been valued for their separate breed status, but there is at least one other breed that competes against the parent whose type it adopted. In the ACA, the Himalayan is no longer a Himalayan—a separate breed of cat, accepted by other organizations. It was created by crossing a Siamese and Persian and should look, in type, like the Persian. Since many Himalayans of fine breeding have achieved this status, in at least one association, they are now considered a different color of Persian. So the Colorpoint Shorthair is not alone in this type of controversy. It will be interesting to see how the years treat such breeds and where they will eventually find their niche. With nine associations, even if two agree there will always be seven more to deal with; and if they all agreed, there would not be nine to begin with and so it goes . . .

In the meantime, the British GCCF accepted the Colorpoint Shorthair in the 1960's as an additional group of colors within the regular Siamese class. A decade earlier, the Colorpoint was recognized by US cat fanciers, but running true to the American spirit of independence, homefront organizations could not agree

Grand Champion Da-Glo's Red Baron, owned and bred by Evelyn Huffman.

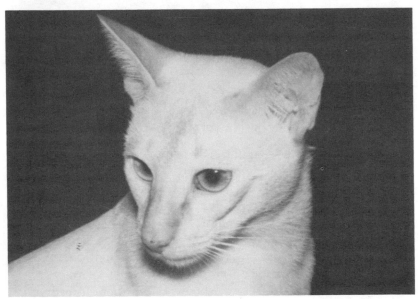

Whiskey Sour of Shemar, a seal lynx point male. He is owned by June Dumanowski. Breeders were Tim and Robin Wood. Photo by Harold Davis.

on an appropriate class for the new breed. Some have placed it with the Siamese, while others have established a completely separate class for it, and so it competes accordingly. Breeders of the Colorpoint do not agree either, polarizing around the same points of dispute as the association.

The Colorpoint's personality resembles that of the Siamese. As for its type—the description is the same as for the Siamese. In judging, the Siamese standard also applies, except for color. According to the standard, the cat should be fine-boned, medium-sized, dainty and svelte with long tapering lines, muscular but lithe. Its head forms a long tapering wedge, medium in size, beginning at the nose and flaring to the tips of the ears. This wedge gives the appearance of a triangle with no break at the whiskers. Space between the eyes should be no less than the width of one eye. The Colorpoint has a flat skull with no bulges in the face and no dip in the nose. Overall, the cat's structure is one of straight lines and flat planes, the head an integral part of this composition. Its nose is long, slender and straight atop a fine, wedge-shaped muzzle. The ears, strikingly large and pointed, are wide at the base continuing the lines of the wedge. The almond-shaped eyes are medium in size. A tight-muscled stomach, same in width as shoulders and hips, creates a tubular looking body set on long, slim legs—hind ones slightly taller than front—ending in dainty, small, oval feet. The long thin tail tapers to a fine point, covered with the same fine-textured, close-lying, glossy, short hair as the rest of the body.

The following colors are acceptable for this cat: red point, cream point, seal lynx point, chocolate lynx point, blue lynx point, lilac lynx point, red lynx point, blue cream point, seal tortie point, chocolate cream point and the lilac cream point. Color descriptions follow elsewhere in the text.

Grand and Double Champion Mor-Ace's Delilah, a silver Egyptian Mau female, owned and bred by Anthony Morace. Photo by Kevin T. Sullivan.

Egyptian Mau

The Egyptian Mau is indeed a natural breed, thought to be descended from the ancient cats of Egypt which were worshipped and held sacred. According to Natalie Troubetskoye, the woman responsible for bringing them into this country, the name Mau is another name for cat and is unnecessary in the name. However, in all associations which accept it as a breed, it is known by this name and will be referred to here as such. It is a pure breed and the only natural breed of spotted domestic cat. Ancient Egyptian art shows cats with such spotting. They were referred to as the spotted "fishing and fowling" cats and must have been great hunters to gain such a name. This is not the only coat pattern shown in ancient Egyptian pictures. There are two varieties of skin pattern. Some have lined markings similar to the Abyssinian while others have the distinctive spotted markings. It is possible that the Abyssinian and the Egyptian Mau are cousins. Both originated in the same place and both are found in ancient art. These perhaps are the oldest and purest of the cat breeds. One of the ancient papers showing this cat is the Egyptian Book of the Dead in which a heavily spotted cat with striped legs and tail is depicted killing a snake. The Ani Papyrus also has examples of spotted cats. The Papyrus of Hunefer from the Book of the Dead is said to portray Ra, the Sun god, in the form of a spotted cat slaying a serpent. This may be the same reference as that above. However, it is known that these cats were closely associated with those worshipped by the Egyptians. Bast, the best known of the gods, representing the life-giving heat of the sun, was depicted as a cat. Reference to her is frequently made in Egyptian history and art, and certainly enters into the history of the cat.

These cats, like the Abyssinian, are believed to be descended from the spotted variety of *Felis lybica* called the *Felis lybica*

International Champion Far East Na Ja, a silver female. Breeder-owners are Jeff and Jean Kryszczuk. Photo by Kel-Den Associates, Inc.

ocreata which came from the highlands of Ethiopia to Egypt. This breed became domesticated and individuals were found in northeastern and southwestern parts of Africa, Italy, Arabia and Libya.

In Europe the Egyptian Mau goes back to 1953. Princess Natalie Troubetskoye was one of the first breeders in Italy. There she saw her first Egyptian Maus, a spayed silver female and a smoke male. They were being used as mascots and were not for sale. But with the help of an ambassador in Rome, she obtained a silver kitten from Cairo called Baba. This cat was bred to the smoke Egyptian Mau, Geppa, and two bronze kittens, Joseph and Jude were the result. Jude died later, but Joseph, known as Jo-Jo, sired a daughter Lisa from Baba and all three were shown at the International Cat Show in Rome in 1954 or 1955. The three cats came to the United States with the Princess in late December, 1956, along with their papers, awards and history. Since the three were recognized by the European registry, CFF registered the cats and they gained championship status with that organization in 1968. Even before that, Lisa was shown at the Empire Cat Show in 1957 as the first Egyptian Mau exhibited in this country. Baba of Fatima, a silver female, became the first champion in America. Several years later CCA accepted the breed. Ch. Kattiwycke's Chale of Hellgate, a bronze male, was the first Canadian champion and the first bronze champion in the US. The Egyptian Mau

Fatima's Figaro, a black smoke specimen. Breeder-owner is Princess Natalie Troubetskoye. Photo by Alice Su.

is now recognized by all associations but ACFA, which gives it provisional status. In CFA it gained acceptance in the championship class as of May 1977.

The personality of this cat is interesting. Members of the breed are reported to have good memories and are basically very loving, though somewhat shy. They tend to attach themselves to one or two people. They love to ride shoulders and will sit and sleep in your lap. They chirp rather like a bird and can be playful and gentle. Built for agility, they are very active cats, easily trained, and often learn tricks by themselves. Despite their builds, they are strong and very muscular.

The breed has a unique appearance. Its basic build is cobby, but similar to the Oriental. It is a colorful cat, of medium size, active with well-developed muscular ability. The head is a modified, slightly rounded wedge, lacking flat planes, and the brow, cheek and profile all show a gentle contour. The muzzle is not pointed. Its ears are alert, large and moderately pointed, broad at the base and upstanding with ample width between them. Hair on the ears is short and close-lying, and the inner ear is a delicate, almost translucent, shell pink that may be tufted. The eyes, large and alert, are almond shaped, slanting slightly upward toward the ears. Its medium length body is graceful, with hind legs longer than the front. It looks as though it were standing on tip-toe when standing upright. Its feet are small and dainty. The tail is medium long, thick at the base and tapering slightly toward the tip. The lustrous coat is silky and fine in texture but dense and resilient to the touch with hair medium in length but long enough to accommodate two or more bands of ticking, separated by the lighter bands. Eye color is light green—gooseberry green—but an amber cast is acceptable. The young cat may be slow to develop eye color and sometimes takes two years to develop body and color.

The color pattern of this cat is fascinating. There should be good contrast between the pale ground color and the deeper markings. The forehead is barred with the characteristic "M" and

Opposite, above: Sangpur Stones, a silver male, owned and bred by Shirley Keenan. Photo by B. Allen.
Opposite, below: Double Champion Mor-Ace's Hephzibah, a bronze female, owned and bred by Anthony Morace. Photo by K. Sullivan.

frown marks, forming lines between the ears which continue down the back of the neck, ideally breaking into elongated spots along the spine. As the spinal lines reach the rear haunches they melt together to form a dorsal stripe which continues along the length of the tail to its tip. The tail is heavily banded with a dark tip. The cheeks are barred with mascara lines; the first starting at the outer corner of the eye and continuing along the contour of the cheek; a second line starts at the center of the cheek and curves upwards, both lines almost meeting below the base of the ear. On the upper chest there are one or more necklaces, preferably broken in the center. The shoulder markings are a transition between stripes and spots. The upper front legs are heavily barred but the markings do not necessarily match. Markings on the body are randomly spotted with variance in size and shape; round, evenly distributed spots being preferred. Spotting patterns on each side may not

The original Egyptian Maus in this country, Baba and Jo-Jo of Fatima. They are owned by Natalie Troubetskoye. Photo by the Whitney Studio.

Khufu Mared of Sangpur, a smoke female, pictured with her kitten. They are owned by Shirley Kennan. Breeder was Barbara Karlson. Photo by Brian Allen.

match but spots should not run together in a broken, mackerel pattern. Haunches and upper hind legs are a transition of spots and stripes, breaking into bars on the thighs and back to elongated spots on the lower leg. Underside of the body should have "vest button" spots; dark in color against the correspondingly pale ground color. The colors accepted for this cat are generally the silver, bronze and smoke, and in some associations the pewter. Color descriptions can be found elsewhere in the text.

Champion Mohawk Sparkle Plenty, a white Exotic Shorthair. The breeder-owners are Mr. and Mrs. Gordon Chandler. Photo by Weston.

Exotic Shorthair

Crossing the Persian and the Domestic Shorthair or the British Shorthair was not an uncommon practice. The English made this cross with their British Shorthairs to gain back a type they had lost when their breeding programs had been disrupted by the war. They then set the type and bred like to like once again, producing the British Shorthair—a separate breed. In America something a little different happened in the cat fancy. The American Shorthair was an accepted breed with its devoted breeders. However, in the early days of the fancy it was obvious that the Persian was the winner at shows and even the lovely Siamese had trouble defeating this cat. So, some American Shorthair breeders began introducing the Persian to their stock to gain a more Persian-looking American Shorthair. The result was a cat that was not American Shorthair and this did not set well with those who were breeding true. In effect, a new breed had been created that was somewhere between the two breeds. The problem was obvious. The American Shorthair people wanted their breed kept true to its standard but now there existed an animal called an American Shorthair that no longer met the standard for that breed.

Jane Martinke in 1966 first suggested a new class for these hybrid cats which were a cross between a Persian and an American Shorthair. These cats were indeed Persian in type but shorthair in coat length with a medium short, dense, plush coat. It was deserving of recognition and it didn't belong in the American Shorthair class. Late in 1966 with the support of Jean Rose a hybrid class was formed for this breed called the Exotic Shorthair. A new standard was drawn up based on the Persian standard for type and these cats were given championship status. At that point any American Shorthair more closely resembling the Exotic Shorthair was allowed to cross over into the new breed, but never to cross

CFA Grand Champion Bon Appetit Roquefort, a blue male, owned and bred by Martie and Bob Fellman.

back and having crossed, it could still maintain its previous awards. In the meantime, the true American Shorthair people began working toward regaining their breed and purifying it for the show ring. Some lines had never been tampered with, others needed to have the touch of Persian bred out to achieve the true standard for this breed. Finally there would be true American Shorthairs again in the ring with no doubt as to ancestry. In 1967-1968 the Exotic was shown for the first time. The breed is indeed unique—the type in a good example is indeed Persian; the coat is short but has the feel of a Persian coat. Their popularity has grown among those admiring the Persian type but liking a shorthair for easier care and other reasons. Many breeders rallied to the new breed and in 1969 Bob and Nancy Lane started the Exotic Shorthair Fanciers. They had been pioneers of the breed and their Leprechaun Cattery had its first grand in Leprechaun's Texas Tea. The first Exotic grand was owned by Kay Campbell (Valentine) and was Silver Secret of Gay-O. Another early grand was Don and Barbara Yoder's Docia-Dao's Patricia and Doris Walkingstick's Grayfire Cheyenne. Many other catteries have bred the Exotic Shorthair since then but these were the first.

At first the crosses for this breed included Persian to American Shorthair and thus the outcome was registered as Exotic, but other breeds were used to some advantage. One of these was the Burmese whose type gave much to the Exotic and whose color didn't seem to bother the breeding program at all. However, in 1975 CFA specified only certain allowable crosses to produce this new hybrid cat. These consisted of an Exotic and Exotic, Exotic and ASH, Persian and ASH and Persian and Exotic. It has been found that the best crosses are between Exotic and Persian. Exotic to Exotic produces good results, but breeding back to the American Shorthair affects type and coat. Naturally, the first generation hybrid comes from the original parents—the American Shorthair and the Persian. The breed was accepted in 1972 by ACFA and then by CFF for championship status.

The Exotic is a cat that loves people, children and other cats, and is bright and alert, but also quiet and gentle. It is not timid

Champion Bon Appetit Black Licorice, a black female. Breeder-owners are Martie and Bob Feldman. Photo by The Camera Box.

and loves to play, but will not be destructive. It is described as sweet and loving and very even-tempered. It is a responsive and intelligent animal. It seems that the combination of Persian—a quiet, loving, docile animal—and American Shorthair—a highly intelligent and responsive cat—is perfect for this cat, giving it a personality that is not extreme, thus making it a wonderful pet.

The Exotic has a round and massive head with great breadth of skull. The face is round and set on a short, thick neck. Its nose is short, broad and has a break. The cheeks are full, the chin full and well developed. The ears are small, round-tipped, tilted forward and not unduly open at the base; they are set far apart and low on

Bon Appetit Buttercream, a cream female, owned by Eleanore Hamling. Breeders were Martie and Bob Fellman.

Champion Mohawk Gem, a copper eyed white. Breeder-owners are Mr. and Mrs. Gordon Chandler. Photo by Grant Weston.

the head, fitting the rounded contour of the head. The eyes are large, brilliant, round and full; they are set far apart, complementing the sweet expression of the face. The body is cobby, low on the legs, deep in the chest, equally massive across the shoulders and rump with a short well-rounded middle section. This cat is large to medium in size with a level back, and short, thick strong legs. The forelegs should be straight and the paws large, round and firm. The tail is short but in proportion to the body and carried without a curve at an angle lower than the back. The coat is medium in length, dense, soft in texture, glossy and full of life.

The Exotic Shorthair is accepted in the following colors—whites (odd-eyed, blue-eyed and copper-eyed), blue, black, red, cream, chinchilla, shaded silver, shell cameo, shaded cameo, black smoke, blue smoke and cameo smoke. The tabby in classic and mackerel pattern in silver, red, brown, blue, cream and cameo. Also tortoiseshell, calico, dilute calico, blue-cream and bi-color.

Quad. Champion Namekagon Sweet-Met, a Havana Brown female. Breeder-owner is Velta G. Dickson. Photo by Larry W. Turner.

Havana Brown

The Havana Brown is another breed not found in a natural state, nor did nature take it into her own hands to create this cat by a spontaneous mutation. Somehow this color had come into being in accidental breedings and people who saw these self-colored brown cats were fascinated with them and became intent on breeding such cats. It is said that in 1894 a brown cat had been shown in England and was called the Swiss Mountain cat and again in 1930 a brown cat was seen by fanciers. Actual work with this cat started officially in 1951.

Certain women must be credited with the creation of this breed. They include the Baroness von Ullmann of Roofspringer Cattery, Mrs. Armitage Hargreaves of Laurentide Cattery, Mrs. Elsie Fisher of Praha Cattery and Mrs. Munro-Smith of Elmtower Cattery. The first chestnut brown kitten produced after much research was born in 1953. This male was believed to be Praha Gypka and resulted from mating a black Shorthair and a chocolate point Siamese. Judging from the prefix, the cat was bred by Mrs. Elsie Fisher. Other breedings took place between Russian Blues and Siamese. However, it should be noted that the year before this designed breeding produced an Havana Brown, one was accidentally produced by Mrs. Munro-Smith who mated a black Shorthair and a sealpoint. Elmtower Bronze Idol, a male self-chocolate was born in 1952 from Susannah, the Shorthair mother and Tombee, the Siamese father. He was the first of the present day Havanas.

Genetically, during the 50's and 60's the recipe for breeding Havanas was to use a Russian Blue or a Shorthair black and mate it to a chocolate point Siamese. The elusive chocolate point gene had to appear in both parents for the Havana to appear. However, when Havanas are bred with other Havanas carrying the blue gene factor, kittens with a pinkish gray coat could result. Such was the case with the first lavender foreign Shorthair bred in England in 1954 by Elsie Fisher who bred Praha Gypka and got this lavender-colored cat which she called Praha Allegro Agitato. Such self-colored lavender kittens also seem to come from Russian Blue mated to chocolate point Siamese. These cats have appeared in the United States and are recognized by several associations.

When the first brown kittens appeared in England it was decided they should be called Havanas because they were the color of rich Havana tobacco and they were registered in the AOV class. In 1958, the required number of generations had been born to gain official recognition for the breed. The GCCF gave it a number, but called the cat the Chestnut Foreign Shorthair. The first English champion, Crossways Honeysuckle Rose, occurred in the early 1960's. It was bred by a Mrs. Judd and owned by Mrs. Davis. In 1970 the name was changed back to Havana. The English found that breeding Havana to Havana for three or more generations lost the foreign type they desired and thus they made crosses back to the chocolate point Siamese to regain type. This is one of the main differences in the Havana and Havana Brown of the United States about which we will see more later.

The first Havanas produced by the English breeders were exported to the United States. Roofspringer Mahogany Quinn, exported by Miss von Ullman to Mrs. Elsie Quinn of California, was the first Havana Brown to become a grand champion in the US and was AW and AA 1960-1964 excluding 1962. Roofspringer Pengo of Chi-Sai was sent to Mrs. Christine Streetman and Revel

Quad. Grand Champion Hamenagon Sweetheart, owned and bred by Velta Dickson. Photo by Larry Turner.

Chestnut Dream of Hi-Fi was sent to Mrs. O'Shea. Laurentide Brown Pilgrim bred by Mrs. Hargreaves was imported to the US by Mrs. J. Peters and another was Revel Chestnut Vision Queuevana owned by Mrs. L. Chastain.

In America the standard was set and accepted by UCF and the Havana Brown was first shown in championship classes at the Siamese Society show in 1959.

The Havana in England is a foreign type cat—actually of Siamese type. The Siamese type in England is not as extreme as ours but the Havana is definitely similar to the Siamese and thus has an Oriental type in England like the Siamese. Thus, the necessity for breeding back to the Siamese to maintain type. However, the Havana Brown in the United States is a separate breed and totally different in type. No crossing back to the Siamese is allowed as no foreign type is desired. By breeding Havana Brown to Havana Brown we have an entirely different type cat than the English Havana which actually is a foreign cat. The English Havana has the long svelte look, the sleek coat, the whip tail and classic, straight profile of a wedge-shaped head. Our Havana Brown has a totally different look as we shall see.

As a pet the cat is highly intelligent, has great ability and moves very fast. It has a need for human companionship and affection. Less vocal than the Siamese, it is hardy and loves to exercise. It is an excellent hunter and loves to play. Affectionate, with a sense of humor and a gentle nature, it makes a good pet.

The Havana Brown has a head slightly longer than it is wide, with a distinct stop at the eyes. Its head narrows to a rounded muzzle with a slight break behind the brown whiskers. The ears are large, round-tipped, with very little hair inside or out; they are wide set, but not flaring. The eyes are chartreuse and oval in shape. The Havana has a body that is medium in length, firm and muscular. Its tail is in proportion to its body and medium in length also. The coat is medium in length and smooth, its color a rich, warm, mahogany brown with the entire coat the same sound shade of brown down to the skin. Nose leather is rosy tone.

Double Champion Ren-Sim's Wedgewood of Theta, a blue point Himalayan male, owned by Alex and Eliza Howard. Breeder was Mary Misner.

Champion and R.M. Quad Ch. Jeanine's Victory of Cat Lore, a seal point Himalayan, owned by Laurie Stevens. Breeder was Henrietta Gray. Photo by Curtis.

Himalayan

The first scientific cross of Siamese and Persian appears to have taken place in Sweden as early as in the 1920's by Dr. K. Tjebbes and in California by Richard Hood. In the early 1930's Dr. Clyde Keeler and Mrs. Virginia Cobb experimented to produce the first recorded Siamese marked cat with long fur. They crossed a Siamese female and a black Persian male. One of the offspring, which were all black Shorthairs, was called Newton's Bozo. They then bred a black Persian female to a Siamese male and again all the kittens were shorthaired blacks. They kept a female from this second litter called Newton's Blitzie. Blitzie was bred to Bozo and produced a longhair black female named Newton's Babbit. This cat mated to Bozo to produce five kittens, one of which was a longhair with colorpoint markings. This occurred in 1935.

The name Himalayan may have come from a Dr. Siegfeld and a Mr. Bernfeld and Susanna Bernfeld who started working toward a longhaired colorpoint and in 1948 the first third-generation kittens were born. They then sold out their cattery to a Mr. Fisher of Forbidden City Cattery. There the story seems to end. In the meantime, Mr. Brian A. Stirling-Webb read about the experiments of Mrs. Cobb and in 1947 was shown a cat of unknown ancestry which was Persian in type with Siamese markings. This cat ended up in his Briarry Cattery and was mated to a black Persian with one Siamese grandparent and this cross produced colorpoint kittens. One of these above mentioned cats most likely the black Persian, may have been produced by Mrs. Barton Wright who in 1935 started the experimental breeder's club and who had produced Himmies from a Siamese male and a blue Longhair female. One female was acquired by Miss Dorothy Collins and was registered Kala Dawn. In 1948 Miss Collins sold Kala Sabu, son of Kala Dawn, to Mr. Stirling-Webb. It is believed that the cat of unknown background was Bubastic Georgina and that she was bred to Kala Sabu, the black Persian that carried a colorpoint gene.

In 1955 GCCF recognized the Colorpoint Longhair that Mr. Stirling-Webb had created with the help of other breeders such as Mrs. Harding, Mrs. Watts and Mrs. Kirby-Smith. Himalayans are known by the name of Colorpoint Longhairs in all parts of the world and shown as another color class of Persian or Longhair except in America where they have a separate class or breed of Himalayan but in which class they must still conform to a Persian standard.

Breeder interest in the US began with several individuals, among them Marguerita Goforth in California who began breeding Himmies about 1950. In addition there were Mr. W.A. Smith of Oregon and Mrs. Flossielu Beer of Colorado who also began to breed for the Himalayan. The first picture of this cat is believed to have been seen in *CATS* magazine. Meanwhile, in Canada, the Borretts were busy working with the Himalayan too. The years 1955, '56 and '57 marked the beginning of recognition for the Himmy in North America. The Borretts showed the first Colorpoint Longhairs, in Alberta, Canada at the ACFA Calgary Cat Show in 1957. These were English imports and were shown in the new breed or color class. Toward the end of 1957 Russell Middletown, founder of ACFA, wrote to the Borretts for a suggested standard. It was presented, published and voted upon in 1957 and in January 1958 after its acceptance, it was published again under the name Himalayan. The name, Himalayan, came from the color pattern of this cat which is also seen in other animals such as the Siamese, rabbits, goats and mice. CFA followed in accepting the breed and then in 1961, ACA, UCF and CFF.

The first record of a champion in the United States (not counting Canada) is said to be an ACFA champion bred by Mrs. Goforth and owned by Price Cross called Goforth's LaChiquita.

These cats are creamy white or off-white at birth with pink noses, paw pads and ears. In a few days a pigment develops in these parts as well as the mask and points beginning to darken as the fur grows. It is believed that darkening in these areas is caused by a temperature factor gene that restricts color to these areas

Double Grand Ch. Ta-Lee-Ho's Bodacious, a seal point Himalayan. Breeder-owner is Sally Geyer.

because blood does not flow to these extremities as readily as it does to the rest of the cat's body.

As a pet the Himmy is intelligent and provocative. It is a combination of the lovely and lazy Persian and the lively and clever Siamese. It has a voice and a bearing more like the Persian. It is devoted to its owner and loves to be fondled and stroked. It is quick to learn and is docile and unique—a combination of oriental beauty in a flowing coat with Persian type. Its popularity leaves no doubt that the combination has been well received.

To make a few things clear, the Himalayan is a man-made breed. It has the coloring (markings) and eye color of the Siamese, one of its original parents, yet its coat, body and face type are those of its

Grand Ch. Hima-Shell Hot Toddy, a tortie point female, owned and bred by Michelle Woods. Photo by Ralph Bork.

Persian parent. Always in the beginning the breeder will find a Persian-to-Siamese breeding produces only shorthaired black kittens because both the longhair gene and the colorpoint gene are recessive. Thus, it has been an uphill battle to produce the lovely cats we see today with the Siamese markings, yet with Persian type and coat. Until 1960 the associations allowed only breeding of Himmy to Himmy if the offspring were to be accepted. But, it was discovered that the cats were not turning out as Persian as the standard called for and the owners desired. For that reason breeders went back to the Persian parent to get more type; and this has been the process for all good show type Himalayans since that time. This process involves a partial genetic link with one of the original parents. A Himmy is bred to a Persian. The result is a litter of all longhaired kittens, as both parents are Longhairs, but because the Persian does not carry the colorpoint recessive gene the hybrid kittens are solid in color. They, however, do carry the gene now for colorpoint in the next generation. When one of these kittens is bred back to a Himmy parent the litter will contain a percentage of colorpoint kittens and a percentage of hybrid kittens that are solid in color but carry the colorpoint gene. Such breeding establishes one thing—type. The Persian used is usually one with very good body and face type and the desired result is a Himalayan that has more Persian type. Therefore, though the Himalayan started as a half and half breed, Siamese to Persian, today it has only the coloring and eye color of the Siamese. It is a Persian in type and for that reason in at least one association to date, this cat has been accepted (as it already is across Europe and in England) as a color class of the Persian. This objective seems to be important to some Himalayan breeders while others wish the cat to remain a separate breed. The Himalayan controversy is similar to that regarding placement of the Colorpoint Shorthair and one that only the future will resolve. Regardless of which class or breed it is judged in at a show, the best Himalayan has the type closest to the Persian and therefore hybrid breeding is important though very time-consuming and involves great selectivity and thorough knowledge of one's lines. The result can be seen in a typical Himalayan grand.

To further make a point, the Himalayan is a hybrid—a cross between two breeds—which will go on its way mostly as a Persian with Siamese coloring. It is no relation to the Balinese and breeders of each breed should take exception to such confusion. The Balinese has long hair, but the coat is unlike the Himalayan's. More importantly the Balinese has the type of the Siamese, in keeping with the objective of the breed, ie. to maintain extreme Siamese type. The Balinese, unlike the Himalayan, is a mutation rather than a hybrid; it simply happened in a litter and was continued by interested breeders. It is hoped that the two are not confused—a good specimen of each side by side would leave little doubt that they bear no resemblance except in eye color and colorpoint markings. Their type and coat are entirely different.

The Himalayan breed forms a class almost as large as the Persian as its popularity grows. There will be those that honor the Himmy to Himmy breeding; others will insist that hybrid breeding is the only answer to Persian type in the Himalayan,which is what the standard calls for. There will be those who will strive for more and more colors to be recognized in the Himalayan class, and new colors are coming on the scene all the time including the chocolate cream (chocolate tortie), seal lynxpoint, the lilac cream, blue lynxpoint, the chocolate smoke, the chocolate and white Bi-colors and the chocolate Calicoes. There are also the selfs. These are cats of a solid color, either

Cat Lore Witchipoo, a seal point female, owned by Marcia Jeffries. Breeder was Laurie Stevens. Photo by Curtis.

chocolate or lilac. In the past they have been used in the breeding of chocolate point and lilac point Himalyans. They are hybrids but some breeders are seeing them as colors in themselves to be judged as other solid-colored cats—in this case in the Persian class since their type is Persian. This has already happened in ACA where chocolate and lilac Persians are accepted. The future holds much in store for the Himalayan. Will it become a Persian or stay a Himalayan?

The Himmy has a round, massive head with great breadth of skull. The face has a well-rounded underlying bone structure. The neck is short and thick. The nose is short and broad with a break and the cheeks are full. The Himmy has a broad powerful jaw and full, well-developed chin. The ears are small, round tipped, tilted forward and not unduly open at the base; they are set far apart and low on the head fitting into the rounded contour of the head. The brilliant, large eyes are round and full, set far apart and give a sweet expression to the face. The cobby body, low on the legs, is deep in the chest and as massive across the shoulders as the rump, with a short well-rounded mid section. The back should be level. The legs are short, thick and strong with straight forelegs and large, round and firm paws. The tail is short and carried without a curve at an angle lower than the back. The coat is long and thick,

Grand Champion Joedeans Earthquake, a seal point male, owned and bred by Joseph Dino Sciorillo.

standing off from the body; it is of fine texture, glossy and full of life. It is long all over the body, including the shoulders; the ruff is immense, continuing in a deep frill to a point between the front legs. Ear and toe tufts should be long and the tail full.

The body color should be free of barring, with only subtle shading allowed. There should be a definite contrast between body color and point color. The points cover the mask, ears, legs, feet, and tail and should be dense and clearly defined. All points should be the same shade and free of barring. The mask covers the entire face including whisker pads and is connected to the ears by tracings. The mask should not, however, extend over the top of the head.

The Himalayan is accepted in the following colors but not necessarily in all associations, and in at least one association the Himalayan is a Persian regardless of color. The accepted colors are the blue point, lilac point, chocolate point, seal point; the flame red (or red point) and the tortie including the seal with red and/or cream, the chocolate with red and/or cream, the blue with red and/or cream and the lilac with red and/or cream; the self chocolate, the self lilac; and the lynxpoint including the red lynxpoint, the lilac lynxpoint, the blue lynxpoint, the chocolate lynxpoint and the seal lynxpoint.

Above: Champion Arlynn Shimon of Mi-Ho, a red and white Japanese Bobtail, owned by Barbara Hodits. Photo by Michael J. Hodits.
Below: Kasi Moto of Juana-Lalo, a male black and white Japanese Bobtail, bred by Dee D. Graff. He is owned by Mr. and Mrs. Edward Skeels.

Japanese Bobtail

The Japanese Bobtail is a natural breed which originated in Japan and roamed its streets quite as our domestic cats do. It is not man-made and it is not a hybrid or mutation. For centuries this type of cat has been seen in Japanese art, in paintings and carvings, woodcuts and statues. There is even a temple in Tokyo that has its facade covered with pictures of these cats with their paws raised, a symbol of good luck. These cats are known in Japan as Mi-Ke cats, and are usually a tri-colored variety, a calico with bold colors and distinctive markings. In Japan they mean good luck and in shop windows or on store counters there are often statues of the tri-colored Mi-Ke cats with one forearm outstretched as an invitation to the passerby. These are called welcoming cats or "Maneki neko." It is believed that the Bobtail will often raise one of its forelegs and hold it outstretched as a sort of greeting.

In Japan and other countries in the Far East including Korea and China they are considered just a domestic cat, but great effort has gone into making the people realize they have a unique breed. But they don't consider it unique because its history in these countries goes back many centuries and Japanese prints show this cat with its distinctive bunny tail in many poses with Japanese ladies.

The credit for bringing this cat to our country goes to Mrs. Elizabeth Freret. It is to this lady that I owe my first acquaintance with this lovely breed and the information that she supplied prior to her death. Though she was well known for her work with other breeds, the Bobtail owes its place in the fancy to this fine woman. She first saw a Bobtail in the US in a pet store where it was being boarded for a family who had just returned from Japan. It was a red tabby spay with a short fluffy tail like a rabbit's. After inquiring about this cat she learned that such cats roamed the streets of

Japan and many had tails as the one she had seen. It seems that at the same time a Judy Crawford had been working with this breed in Japan for some time. She sent the first Japanese Bobtails to Mrs. Freret in 1968. One of the kittens was a calico—a Mi-Ke. Her name was Mme. Butterfly. There was also a red and white male named Richard. A third cat came too, a cinnamon colored tabby female that did not stay with Mrs. Freret. Butterfly was eventually bred to Richard and the kittens had tails identical to their parents and they were also as vividly colored. In 1969 Mrs. Freret took Butterfly and her kittens to a CFA meeting. The breed was accepted for registration. In May, 1971 it was accepted for provisional status and in May of 1976 it was accepted for championship competition but Mrs. Freret did not live to see this.

It is important to note that the Bobtail is not a relative of the Manx, which has no tail whatsoever. The Bobtail, on the other hand, has always been shown with a tail that is crooked and often described as looking like a bunny's tail. The tail is about two inches long and then has a fallen-over, broken effect which is allowed. The whole tail appear as to be rigid with a one-piece bone rather than a jointed tail with vertebrae like most. The Bobtail carries its tail high like a banner or flag. The hair is longer and thicker on the tail than the rest of the body and grows outward giving a pompom effect. There may be one or more broken ninety degree angles.

In breeding, the Bobtail is produced by a simple recessive gene. Two Bobtailed cats will produce all Bobtail kittens although some may have tails which are a bit too long but they make excellent breeders. Bobtails to domestics will produce normal tails. No outcrossing is allowed with the Bobtail. The breed is accepted in different combinations of the colors that make up the Mi-Ke, black, red and white; black and white, red and white, and tri-colors such as black, red and cream (tortoiseshell) or black, red and white or tortie and white.

The Japanese Bobtail is a people cat and very outgoing. They develop strong ties, do not like to be caged and adapt quickly and easily. They are intelligent quiet cats, but can be very conversational when they want. It has been said that they like to retrieve, are great swimmers and love water. They are friendly and sociable and may well welcome visitors with that characteristic wave of the paw. They tend to speak in different tones and to chirp, hum, meow and talk to their owners and to other cats. Breeders make note of their clannishness. They like other cats, but given the choice will seek out their own breed to be with.

The Japanese Bobtail has a head that appears long and finely chiseled; it forms an almost perfect triangle with gentle curving lines, high cheek bones and a noticeable whisker break. The nose is long and well defined by two parallel lines from tip to brow with a gentle dip at, or just below, eye level. The ears are large, upright and expressive, set wide apart but at right angles to the head rather than flaring outward, and give the impression of being tilted forward in repose. The muzzle is fairly broad, neither pointed nor blunt, and rounding into the whisker break. The eyes are large, oval rather than round, but wide and alert. They are set into the skull at a rather pronounced slant. The body is medium in size, long and lean, but shapely and well muscled. The legs are long, slender and high, but not dainty and fragile in appearance. The hind legs are longer than the forelegs but deeply angulated or bent when the cat is standing relaxed so that the torso remains nearly level rather than rising toward the rear. When standing, the cat's forelegs and shoulders form two continuous straight lines, close together. The coat is medium length, soft and silky but without a noticeable undercoat. The tail should be no more than two to three inches from the body even though if straightened out it might be longer. The tail is usually carried upright when the cat is relaxed. Hair on the tail is somewhat longer and thicker than on the body, growing outward in all directions to create a pom pom or bunny tail effect which appears to commence at the base of the spine, camouflaging the underlying bone structure of the tail. The tail bone is usually strong and rigid rather than jointed (except at the base) and may either be straight or composed of one or several curves and angles.

Grand Champion Jesilieu's Kukrit of Solna, a Korat male, owned by Sonia Megan Anderson. Breeder was Jessalee Mallabieu. Photo by MikRon Photos.

Korat

There is an ancient book on view in the National Library in Bankok showing cats in picture and verse. Known as the *Cat Book Poems*, it dates from the Ayudhya Period of Thai history (1350-1767). Among the cats depicted are the sealpoint Siamese, the copper (Burmese) and the silver blue cat of Thailand, the Korat, or Si-Sawat, as it is generally known in Thailand.

At the turn of the century, a highranking monk was commissioned by King Rama V (King Chulalongkorn) to paint a copy of this book. It is on view in the National Museum in Bangkok, and is known as the "Smud Khoi."

The poem in reference to the Korat, or Si-Sawat, goes:
"The cat 'Maled' has a body colour like 'Doklao'.
The hairs are smooth, with roots like clouds and tips
    like silver.
The eyes shine like dewdrops on a lotus leaf."

'Maled' means seed and refers to the seed of the Look Sawat, a wild fruit in Thailand with a silvery gray seed that is tinged with green. 'Dok' means flower and lao is a kind of herb with silvery tipped flowers. 'Si-Sawat' is a compound Thai word meaning a mingled color of gray and light green. Therefore, because of the associations and meanings of its name, Korats are silver blue from birth to death. A cat of any other color is not a Korat.

King Chulalongkorn is credited with naming the Korat. It is said that he commented on the beauty of one of these cats and asked where it came from. When the owner replied, "From Korat", they became known as Korat cats. It is presumed they meant the Korat Province of Thailand. They are rare in Thailand but can be found in this province and others too where they are highly prized for their beauty and for the good luck they are believed to bring to their owners. A pair of them is a traditional gift to a bride, symbolizing a gift of silver, bringing prosperity and a fortunate marriage. One of these cats is sometimes used in rain-making ceremonies. It has been referred to as the cloud-colored cat with eyes the color of young rice, bringing the promise of good crops to the farmer. The Thai prize these cats and rarely sell them. At one time they were given only as a token of honor or esteem. A few accounts of Korats being seen in Thailand may be found in books by cat authorities but little has been documented of their appearance in the western countries. In 1896, at the National Cat show at Holland House in London, we are told that a young Mr. Spearman exhibited a Korat. The judges called it a blue Siamese. Mr. Spearman defended it and said there were many in Thailand from where he had brought it.

In 1959, the first Korats known to have been used for breeding arrived in America, sent to Mrs. Robert W. (Jean) Johnson by a friend. Some years earlier, 1947, she had learned about these cats during a stay in Thailand. While searching for the Siamese cat, she was shown the Korat and told it was the true Thai cat. In 1959 her friend had sent a pair of these Thai cats, Korats, obtained from the famed Mahajaya line bred by Mme. Ruen Abhibal Rajamaitri of Bangkok. Their names were Nara and Darra. Their mother, Mom Noel, was born in Korat and brought to Bangkok. In 1962, Mahajaya Dok Rak and Nai Sri Sawat Miow from Cholburi Province were brought to America by Gail Lankenau (now Woodward). Mrs. Gertrude Gecking (now Sellars) visited Bangkok and purchased Me Luk, born in October 1963, from Mr. Chompoo.

In May of 1965 a small group of founder members formed an unaffiliated breed society, naming it the Korat Cat Fanciers Association. Much groundwork in getting the breed better known had been laid by Jean Johnson and those who had heard or read about her lovely new breed from Thailand and purchased cats from her. Among these were Mr. and Mrs. Ray Gardner, who started breeding Korats in California in 1963. Daphne Negus, Secretary for the Association, sent a questionnaire to all known Korat breeders and owners. From the replies, a proposed standard was compiled by Mr. and Mrs. Gardner and Mrs. Negus, based on the official CFA standard requirements. The standard was sent back to all participants for their approval. It was taken to shows, exhibits,

A foursome of perky Korat kittens, owned and bred by Esther Epstein. Photo by L.M. Buckingham.

seminars and teas where the members were bringing their Korats and advice and comments were sought from judges and breeders all through America, Canada and Thailand. In October 1965, it was submitted to all the cat registering associations with a presentation requesting championship status for the breed.

The breed was accepted in America by ACA, NCFA and UCF in April; by CFA in September; in Canada by CCA in October; by ACFA in February 1967; by CFF in 1968; and by Crown in January 1969. Korats first competed in championship classes in June 1966 in the ACA King of Prussia show in Pennsylvania. In South Africa, Korats were recognized in January, 1968; in Australia in July, 1969; and in England by the GCCF in February 1975.

No Korat is a Korat unless it can trace its ancestry back to Thailand. Papers necessary to get the cat into this country are many: rabies and enteritis vaccination certificates, airway bill or ship's manifest, customs receipt at the port of entry, and pedigree. According to Daphne Negus who visited Bangkok in 1968, bringing back nine of the total of thirteen Korats she has personally imported into America, this cat should be called "the cat with a passport."

The Korat Cat Fanciers Association is dedicated to the protection and development of the Korat cat. Cats are sold with KCFA sales contract/pledge signed by the seller and buyer which guarantees that the cat is of Thai ancestry and is sold exactly as represented, show quality or pet quality. The buyer agrees to protect the cat's health, never to breed it with another breed, to call

Grand and Triple Champion Si Sawat's Sunan, male, owned by Richard negus. Breeder was Mrs. Richard Negus. Photo by Warren Gorman.

Double Grand Champion Caran's Saidi of Thata-Gata, female, owned by Esther Epstein. Photo by Buckingham.

the offspring Korats, and never to deal with pet shops or animal dealers. Pets are promised to be altered and papers are presented when they are altered. KCFA publishes a newsletter quarterly called *Mai Pen Rai* (My Pen Rye) which means a happy philosophy of "It doesn't matter . . . never mind," hoping its members will never take themselves so seriously that they lose sight of their prime interest—the welfare of the cats. This club also presents its own awards annually for championship and premiership cats, and ribbons are given out for the Best Korat to shows that request them. Annual awards are listed in the newsletter. By means of the KCFA census forms, maintained and circulated by the breeders, pairing of bloodlines is possible with leads on available kittens, stud service and cats. KCFA keeps records of all imports. There is also the Si-Sawat Society and the Sah What Dee, both CFA affiliated, plus the Korat Fanciers of the East, affiliated with CFF. England, too, has a very active club, named the Korat Group.

As pets, the Korats love to be fondled and to engage in vigorous

A cozy twosome, Ch. Miz-Liz Chinda of Thata-Gata and Ch. Miz-Liz Sarai of Thata-Gata, owned by Esther Epstein. Breeder was Kathryn Robert. Photo by Buckingham.

play. They have good senses and are gentle pets. They move slowly and cautiously, disliking sudden, loud and harsh noises. They form strong relations with their owners and like other cats and kittens too. They do like their own breed and will seek them out before a different breed. They are smart and enjoy playing but are not destructive. They talk little except for a greeting or signal for food. They are, all in all, intelligent, intuitive, gentle, cautious, agile and swift in movement.

The Korat has a heartshaped head with breadth between and across the eyes, the eyebrow ridges forming the upper curves of the head, and the sides of the face gently curving down to the chin to complete the heart shape. Between the nose and the forehead is a slight stop and the tip of the nose just above the leather has a lion-like downward curve. The chin and jaw are strong and well developed, not overly square or too sharply pointed, nor should the chin be weak, making the face look pointed. The ears are large with a rounded tip and large flare at the base; they are set high on the head, giving an alert expression. Hair inside the ears is sparse and on the outside is extremely short and close. The body is semi-cobby, that is neither short-coupled like the Manx nor long like the Siamese; it is muscular, supple with a feeling of hard-coiled spring power and unexpected weight; the back is carried in a curve. Males should look powerful and fit and females should be smaller and dainty. Medium and curved describe the body size and shape. The legs are in proportion to the body and the distance from the base of the neck to the base of the tail appears to be equal to the distance from the base of the tail to the floor. The front legs are slightly shorter than the back legs. The paws are oval. The tail is medium in length, heavier at the base, tapering to a rounded tip. The eyes are large and luminous; they are particularly prominent, with extraordinary depth and brilliance, wide open and oversized for the face. The eye opening when fully open is well rounded but when closed has an Asian slant. Eye color is a luminous green with an amber cast accepted. Eye color development takes as long as four years.

The cat has a single-layered coat with hair that is short to medium in length, glossy and fine, and lies close to the body. The hair does not float off when stroked. Coat color is silver blue all over, tipped with silver, the more silver tipping the better. It is without shading or markings. Where the coat is short, the sheen of the silver is intensified. Nose leather is dark blue or lavender as are the paw pads.

Maine Coon

The Maine Coon cat originated in the United States over a hundred years ago and is a natural breed native to this country and particularly to its home state of Maine. Legends concerning this cat are numerous and its history is sketchy, going from popularity to obscurity and back again. Some say this cat originated in the wilds of Maine due to a cross between a Domestic Shorthair and a raccoon—thus the name Coon cat, but this would be genetically impossible. There is also the romantic legend that Marie Antoinette, planning to make her escape during the hard times in France, sent her cats to a special place in Maine to be hidden for her. What is the truth of the matter?

One theory has been that the cat is a result of an Angora, believed to be the first Longhair to reach our shores, and a Domestic. This is possible. A new belief is that the cat is a cross between a Domestic and an American Bobcat. Regardless, we have the Maine Coon whose colors, body structure and uneven coat point to several factors basic to this cat. It was free-roaming and in the rugged Maine country for years, developing a rugged coat and constitution able to withstand the rigors of that environment. Its behavior has been described by owners as reflecting a cat that spent time in the wilds, and I suppose that its raccoon-like antics add substance to that legend. The wide variety of colors is due to its free-roaming and breeding habits plus its having been fathered (or mothered) by a Domestic. A wide range of solids, particolors and tabbies occur within the normal color patterns of this cat making it unique at a show. Few will look alike in their color and color patterns.

Opposite: Triple Champion All Saints Christa of Lyb-E, a female tortie Maine Coon, owned by Elizabeth H. Broach and bred by Delanne DuBois.

Above: Quad. Grand Champion, International, Quintriple and Quadruple Ch. More-Ace's Satan, a brown tabby male, owned and bred by Anthony Morace. Photo by Kevin T. Sullivan.
Below: Jonlyn's Boston Blackie, owned and bred by John and Jacquelyn Grant.

Overleaf:

Above, left: *Grand Champion Kidar's Silver Pearl, a Persian, owned by Bettijane Myjak and bred by Mr. and Mrs. Jim Romano.*

Above, right: *Two ruddy Somali male kittens, left, L'Air de Rauch's Boo, owned by Mr. and Mrs. John Moore; and right, L'Air de Rauch Rocky Raccoon of Foxtail, owned by Patricia Warren. Both kittens were bred by Mrs. M. Rauch. Photo by Manny Greenhaus.*

Center, left: *A Ragdoll kitten owned by Mrs. Morris Epstein. Photo through the courtesy of Ann Baker.*

Below, left: *Persian kittens, left, Double Grand Champion Willow Lane Precious; right, Willow Lane Little Bit, owned and bred by Isabel Roberts. Photo by Blair Studio.*

Below, right: *Double Champion Mor-Ace's Bettie Joe, a brown tabby Maine Coon, owned and bred by Anthony Morace. Photo by Kevin T. Sullivan.*

Overleaf:

Helen Gamon's Chartreux, Champion Taquin de St. Pierre, bred by Madame S. Bastide. Photo by Tony Francis.

Overleaf:

Camotop's Chandra of Niacus, a lilac point Balinese kitten, owned by Carolyn Jennings and bred by Carol Board.

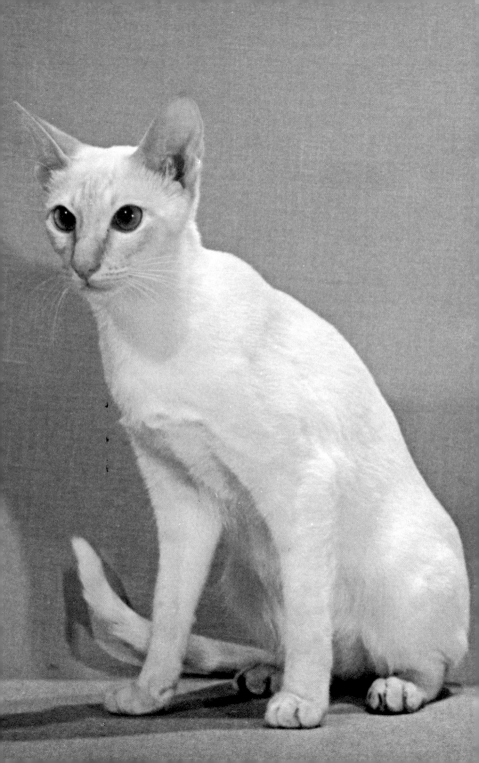

Overleaf:

A red point Colorpoint, Grand Champion J-Bar's Red Silk of JoRene, owned by Dr. Irene B. Horowitz and bred by Mr. and Mrs. Jack Collins. Photo by Larry Levy.

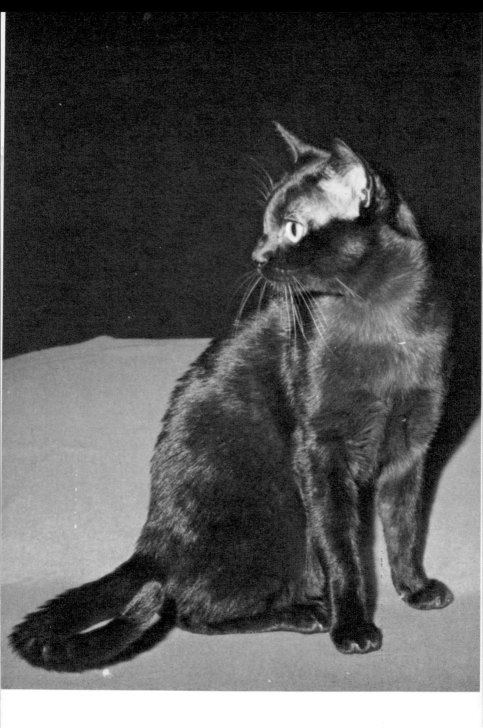

Overleaf:

A trio of Rex kittens, bred and owned by Ber-nadette A. Madden.

Overleaf:

Grand Champion Byken Dee's Demitu, a blue eyed white Rex female, owned and bred by Mr. and Mrs. George Q. Thornton. Photo by Larry Levy.

Overleaf:

Mr. and Mrs. George Q. Thornton's white Rex female, the blue eyed Grand Champion Byken Dee's Demitu.

Overleaf:

Above: *A lilac point Siamese, Grand Champion Jo Rene Gantanol, owned and bred by Dr. Irene B. Horowitz.*

Below: *Grand Champion Gallantree's Casey Jones, a ruddy male Abyssinian owned and bred by Mr. and Mrs. Ron Bauer. Photo by Curtis.*

Overleaf:

Saint Lambert Viviane, a chestnut female Oriental Shorthair, owned and bred by Valeria Zlatkowsky. Photo by Buzzini, Paris, France.

Overleaf:

Patapaw Halle Kelea of Tintadel, right, and Tintadel's Lancelot Du Lilac, left, two lavender Oriental Shorthair males. Both cats are owned by Erica Mueller and bred by Marilyn Buchanan. Photo by Burlington Studios.

Overleaf:

Above, left: *Egyptian Mau kittens, Fatima's Boris, left, and Fatima's Babochka, owned and bred by Princess Natalie Troubetskoye. Photo by Alice Su.*

Above, right: *Grand and Triple Champion Amadear Dorion of Cinemor, a ruddy Abyssinian male, owned by Margot Mor, and bred by Dr. and Mrs. Duane E. Young. Photo by Larry Levy.*

Below, left: *Double Grand Champion and Grand Champion Amadear Orianna, a ruddy Abyssinian female, bred by Dr. and Mrs. Duane E. Young. Photo by Kevin P. Mahoney.*

Center, right: *Shamba Letu Meiko of Grenouille Mi-Ke, a calico Japanese Bobtail female, owned by Mr. and Mrs. Gil Belanger and bred by Carolyn McLaughlin.*

Below, right: *A ruddy Abyssinian male, Grand Champion Crescent Bouhaki of Graymar, owned by Margaret C. Gray, and bred by Dr. Henrietta N. Shirk.*

At first the cat was seen mostly in Maine and highly favored there, but it found its way into other parts of the country as people noted its beauty and took it home from vacation spots in Maine. In addition to its ruggedness, its ability to adapt to the harsh Maine climate, and its raccoon-like antics, the Maine Coon came to be a working cat in this country before it was a show cat. It was part of the family, but also a hunter of rodents, working for its keep. The popularity of the cat is strange in that it grew, flourished and sank into obscurity, then made a strong comeback to its current status of popularity. Perhaps its first wave of popularity was because there were so few native breeds in this country when the cat fancy began and when the exotic breeds were imported the domestic cats were left behind.

The first sign of the Coon on the records was in 1861, the date mentioned by F.R. Pierce of Maine, in the *Book of the Cat* regarding a black and white Longhair he and his brother owned called Captain Jenks of the Horse Marines. The Coon was popular in the late 1800's and in the 1903 *Book of the Cat* by Frances Simpson a chapter was devoted to the breed. Even before this it is believed that cat shows were held in conjunction with fairs and that these cats were shown. In 1895 a tabby Maine Coon was Best Cat at the New York City, Madison Square Garden show and at the same show a brown tabby Coon, Cosie, won awards as a neuter. Cosie was owned by Mrs. E.N. Baker and was bred by E.R. Pierce. King Max, also bred by E.R. Pierce won at the Boston Shows of 1897, 1898, and 1899. However, after 1904 the breed dropped out of sight. In Maine, though, they did not go unnoticed by such people as Ruby Dyer of Skowhegan and Mrs. Robert Whittemore of Augusta, who helped the Coon cat to survive. In 1953 the Central Maine Coon Cat Club was established and they held shows just for Maine Coons. In the mid 1960s people once again became interested in them and registered them beginning with CFF, ACA, CCA, ACFA and NCFA. In 1967 a standard was drawn up and accepted by CCA and ACFA and ACA. Another group called the Maine Coon Breeders and Fanciers Association was formed to aid in the advancement of the Coon cat. The cats have been accepted for registration and show throughout the fancy including CFA and are now becoming a substantial class at shows.

The head on this breed is medium in width and in length with a

Double Champion Mor-Ace's Bettie Joe, a brown tabby, owned and bred by Anthony Morace. Photo by Kevin T. Sullivan.

squareness to the muzzle. The cheekbones are high, the chin firm and in line with the nose and the upper lip. The nose is medium in length. The ears are large, well-tufted, wide at the base and tapering to appear pointed; they are set high and well apart. The eyes are large and wide set. The neck is medium long and its body is muscular, with a broad chest. The size should be medium to large with females smaller than males. The body is expected to be long and with all parts in proportion to create a rectangular appearance.

The Maine Coon has a unique personality. It loves to sleep in strange and awkward places and positions. They use their paws a lot, do tricks and love to play with water, which they will cup in their paws or cause to swirl in their water dish so they can watch it move. They also use their paws in eating. Their voice is unique—no two Coon cats sound alike according to one well-known breeder. They all have a different sound. From what I have observed myself, they are alert-looking, very friendly and outgoing. There is a look in their eyes that says they like people and love fun. For all-around adaptability, personality and ease of grooming, plus tops in amusement and affection, the Coon is a perfect pet. Owners say the cat has another plus—it is a perpetual kitten despite its age and remains very active throughout its life. In the showring it stands out as unique, not only for its type but also in color and color pattern, all making for a cat that reflects its natural heritage.

The legs are substantial, wide set and of medium length with large, round, well tufted paws. The tail is long, wide at the base and tapering with the fur long and flowing. The coat is heavy and shaggy, shorter on the shoulders and longer on the stomach and britches. A frontal ruff is desirable. The coat should be a silky texture, falling smoothly along the cat's sides.

This cat is slow in developing and will not reach its full maturity until about four years of age. It is accepted in the following colors: white, black, blue, cream, classic and mackerel tabby in the silver, red, brown, blue, and cream. Tabbies with white, tortoiseshell, tortoiseshell with white, calico, blue-cream and bi-color.

The eye color in these cats is not related to the coat color and should be shades of green, gold or copper though white cats may also be either blue or odd-eyed.

Above: Manxamumm Jim Dandy, a red mackerel tabby Manx, owned and bred by Jean Mumm.
Below: Grand Champion Kellogg Maredydd, a tortie Manx female, owned and bred by David and Elree Kellogg.

Manx

There are many legends involving the Manx and I suppose it is best to cover those first for the romantics among us who prefer to believe in legends rather than in probability. The legend that the Manx came to the Isle of Man, its established home, due to a shipwreck from the Spanish Armada of 1588 is one of the most popular. However, there is no evidence of tailless cats in Spain and neither is there any record of such a wreck in such a place. The second legend has it that on this island the warriors favored cats' tails as plumes for their helmets and took to using them at the risk of the cat's life. The mother cats (depending on the legend) either took to biting off the tails of their kittens when they were born to avoid this, finally causing all kittens to be born sans tail, or they simply stopped producing kittens with tails in order to save their kittens' lives.

The legend of Noah and the Ark is also charming but hardly believable. According to this account, the Ark was ready to leave and the cats had not arrived. Noah was just about to close the Ark door when in they strolled in an unconcerned and totally independent manner. The gate swung shut on their tails leaving them tailless and causing them to produce only tailless offspring for all time. This does not explain how we now have tailed cats today. Another legend concerns a superstition on the Isle of Man. The Celts supposedly believe that if you tread on the tail of a cat a viper will issue forth and destroy you. Tailed cats somehow weren't popular with this belief abiding in the land. A miracle caused tailless cats to occur and the Celts then took over and perpetuated this breed so they could walk across the island without fear. So much for legends. They are charming but quite untrue.

In point of fact, the Manx appears to have been a mutation that occurred on the island and thus became a new breed because of the closed environment. The gene is believed to be an incomplete dominant and if this mutation had occurred in a less restricted environment it might have been lost. Other characteristics accompany taillessness which proclaim the Manx to be Manx. Outcrossing to other breeds would not lose the taillessness altogether but would alter the other characteristics such as the heavy bones, solid cobby body, long hind legs, powerful hindquarters, large expressive eyes and dense, double coat. Therefore, the general feeling is that this mutation took place on the Isle of Man and became an established breed there, looking at the time the same as we see it today. This island is located in the Irish Sea between the coasts of England and Ireland.

Some say the Manx is related to the Oriental cats and was seen in the time of Marco Polo; that they are great mousers, and would make good ship cats. Actually, genetically, they are not like the Oriental cats which are peculiar in their tail formation, but which *do* have tails. Dr. Neil Todd in 1960 noted distinctions between the two breeds: the Oriental cats have tails that are twisted or hooked but they always possess the last coccygeal bone and even if it is bent, its just being there makes the Oriental breeds very different from the Manx. Another belief held is that the Manx resulted from a cross to a rabbit, thus explaining its hopping gait. This is likewise false. Such a breeding is not possible and the hopping gait is not normal except when the cat is running. If the cat hops when walking it is usually the result of compensation for incomplete control of the muscles in its hind quarters. The Manx is a Manx because of the lack of the coccygeal vertebra that is the beginning of the tail. The completely tailless Manx will carry a dimple on its back where the tail should begin. On the island the Manx is called a Rumpy because of its high rump and short back. They mean good fortune to the Celts and can be found on jewelry, coins and paintings, which shows they are held in high esteem. They seem to have been noticed on the island no earlier than 1820 for sure. On the island in 1960 the Manx Parliament set up a government-owned cattery, the Isle of Man, to provide breeding stock for those who wanted to import a Manx as many of our breeders have. Some believe that all true Manx come from the Isle or at least from England. In 1964 the Douglas Corporation took over and now maintains the cattery and cats may be imported from the Isle of Man. This protects these cats from being taken as

Double Grand and Triple Champion Couer De Lion's Sisie of Mor-Ace, a black and white owned by Anthony Morace. Breeder was Robert Ford Jr. Photo by Kevin T. Sullivan.

ship's cats or by tourists as pets. Before this the Manx population was dwindling due to such losses.

In this country the Manx was first brought to significant notice in the show world about 1933 by Ellen and Ruth Carlson of Glen Orry Cattery. Guthred of Manx of Glen Orr, a red tabby, is believed to have been the first grand champion, receiving its grand in 1951. There have been many more since. The breed has a small but enthusiastic popularity and it has been written that no less than King Edward the VIII of England owned a Manx when he was Prince of Wales.

Genetically, the breed is fascinating. There are five types of Manx, actually, that can appear in a litter. The Rumpy, which is tailless; the Riser which has a small number of vertebrae which

Grand Champion Kelsa Angel 1, a copper eyed white female. Breeder-owner is Judith Shaw.

Grand Champion Kelsh Angeli 3 of Poco-Lina, a brown tabby female, bred by Judith Shaw.

can be felt or seen; the Stubby in which a distinct and movable short tail is present; the Longy which has a longer tail than the rest but still not of normal length, and the Tailed. Many breeders agree that breeding the true Manx (Rumpy to Rumpy) for more than three generations can cause problems. They do not agree as to what type of Manx should be used to offset this. Some say the Stubby, Riser, Longy or even a Tailed Manx will produce good Rumpy kittens with good type and that it is safer than Rumpy to Rumpy endlessly. Others say a good extreme Rumpy and a normally tailed Manx produces more healthy Rumpy kittens. It seems to be true that outcrossing from the Rumpy to Rumpy is necessary. It also appears to hold true that the percentage of Rumpy kittens is better with a Rumpy to Rumpy breeding or a Rumpy to Riser breeding and that the Rumpy and Riser have the best type. With the use of the Stubbies and Longies or the Tailed Manx it is harder to get a large percentage of Rumpy Manx. Every breeder has his own formula. The true show Manx is completely tailless and even in a Rumpy to Rumpy breeding there is a percentage of approximately one third tailed kittens born. It is known for sure that one parent must carry some form of Manx tail, be tailless, or be bred to a tailless cat to produce a Manx kitten. A tailed cat, even from Manx parents, cannot produce tailless or partially tailed kittens if the mate has a full tail too.

As a pet the Manx often attaches itself to one person. They like children, are eager to please and so are easy to train. They are said

Grand Champion Briar Brae Sugar of Daphne, a red classic tabby male, owned by Donna Jewell and Elree Kellogg. Breeder was Barbara St. George.

to be gentle, affectionate and intelligent, not readily forgetting abuse or indifference. They are basically quiet and will chirp softly for attention. They have great courage and are strong and hardy. They love to play and make excellent hunters. They use judgement, seemingly to choose what they like. They should be approached quietly or they might frighten or not have the time to size up a newcomer properly before deciding if it is friend or foe. The Manx makes a unique and loving pet that will be part of the family and loyal even to the point of protecting its owner, but newcomers often need time to be accepted. This is a sensitive and intelligent animal.

The Manx has a fairly round head with prominent cheekbones and a jowly appearance. The head is medium in length and in profile has a definite nose dip. The muzzle is broad and round. The ears are triangular and rather wide at the base, tapering slightly to a point and tilted forward and outward. The eyes are large, round and full. The body is solid and compact and with a back showing a definite rounded incline from the shoulders to the haunches. It is medium in size. The body has great depth, adding to the cobbiness. An absolute specimen has a hollow at the end of the backbone where a tail would begin. A rise of the bone at the end of the spine is allowed as long as it does not stop the flow of the back, which is sturdy and short and conforms in size to the cat. The legs are of good substance, with the front legs short and set well apart to show the good depth of the chest. The back legs are much longer with a heavy, muscular thigh tapering to a substantial lower leg. The paws are small, neat and well rounded. The coat is short, of good texture, with a well padded, quality rising from the longer, hard, glossy outer coat and the thicker cottony undercoat known as the "double coat." The Manx comes in the following colors: the blue-eyed white, the copper-eyed white, the odd-eyed white, the blue, black, red, cream, chinchilla, shaded silver, black smoke, the classic and mackerel tabby in the silver, red, brown, blue and cream, the tortoiseshell, calico, dilute calico, blue-cream, bi-color and other Manx colors known as OMC. Color descriptions can be found in the Color Standard chapter.

Above: Champion Helle's Comus Jupiter, a copper eyed white Manx
Longhair, or Cymric, owned and bred by Blair O. Wright.
Below: Gentibelle Foxhaven, a black and white kitten. Breeder-owner
is C.M. Folz Brown. Photo by Morgan Kaye.

Manx Longhair

This is a mutation from a litter of normal shorthaired Manx with no longhairs in the pedigree. These cats were first born to Manx parents with seven or more generations of pure shorthaired Manx. It was not a mixture of Manx and any longhair breed! Mutations always produce mutations and so it is with the longhaired Manx. Shorthair is dominant over Longhair and thus two Longhair Manx would have to produce all Longhair Manx kittens, because a recessive gene when present in both parents, produces all Longhaired Manx. The initial mutation when bred to another of its kind will breed true. As with mutations, some change one aspect of the cat, some change more than one. In the case of the Rex both type and coat was changed. In the case of the Balinese only the coat length was affected. This is the same with the Longhair Manx which has the same type as the Manx, its parent breed, but has long hair instead of short hair. The coat instead is medium long with fur slightly softer than the shorthaired Manx, but still has the features of the shorthaired Manx, however, in being an open, double coat. The coat does not mat and is easily kept in show condition. As with the Manx the genetics are the same except for this recessive gene for longhair. The longhaired Manx may be born without a tail at all, with a stump or with a tail that is longer but not quite normal length. Since it is a mutation its personality is much like the Manx. They tend to be family cats or belonging to one person. They don't take to strangers easily. They have a high degree of intelligence and a soft, often voiceless meow.

The breed is becoming more popular all the time but I long remember the Lovebunny Cattery which for so many years has had longhaired Manx in the AA listings and Althea Frahm who has worked with this breed for so many years. Now we see catteries with this breed and even Manx breeders who now are showing or selling to be shown their longhaired Manx, though they have long been known only for the shorthaired variety. The breed has been accepted by certain associations including the ACA and CCA who call it by the name of Cymric (pronounced Kim-rick), an old Welsh name meaning simply "Welsh." It is used only in Canada.

What appears to have happened genetically with the Manx is that the awn-coat of the Manx mutated. It was lengthened as with the Balinese and the Somali. Again, there was no cross with a Persian or any other longhair breed. This would not produce the same coat or maintain the other physical characteristics which make the Manx what it is. I am sure the breed will continue to gain acceptance and I give credit to Ms. Frahm and her Lovebunny Cattery and to those just coming on the show scene with this combination of beautiful type and lovely coat resulting in a new breed.

The head of this cat is slightly longer than broad, yet fairly round. High cheekbones are prominent. The muzzle has a whisker break and the nose is longer and broader than the American Shorthair with no suggestion of being snipey and straight when viewed from the side with the fur flattened. The eyes are large, almost round and full with the outer corners set higher than the inner corners. The eye color is of secondary importance and to count only when all other points are equal. The ears are medium in size, rather wide at the base, tapering gradually to a rounded tip; they are wide spaced and set slightly outward. Ear tufts may be present at the tips. The neck is short, thick and well muscled. The body is stout and compact, medium in size with a short back that rises up from the shoulders to the rump. There is a good depth to the chest. The bone is sturdy and the round rump is higher than the shoulders. The greater depth of flank than that of other breeds adds to the short appearance of the cat. This depth of flank, the height of the hindquarters, the shortness of the back and forelegs and the roundness of the rump produce the hopping gait typical of the Manx when running. The legs are heavy set and the forelegs set well apart. The forelegs are short and great depth of chest is seen between the legs. The hind legs are much longer with heavy, muscular thighs tapering to a substantial lower leg, straight when viewed from behind. The feet are round and firm. The roundness of the rump is emphasized by the absence of a visible tail. Sometimes the coccyx (last vertebra) can be felt as a slight rise but should not be penalized unless the round appearance is spoiled. There may be a hollow at the coccyx called a "dimple" but absence is not to be penalized. The coat is double, soft, well-padded, medium-long, full and even, giving a heavier appearance to the body. Long hair on the rump may give the appearance of a short tail.

The same colors are accepted in the longhair Manx as in the shorthair Manx (see preceding section).

For color descriptions refer to the Color Standard section at the rear of the book.

Bev-Len Sparkle-N-Star, a male lavender Oriental Shorthair, owned and bred by Mrs. Beverly Reedy. Photo by Larry W. Turner.

Oriental Shorthair

The Oriental Shorthair is one of the newer breeds in this country, but its cousin, the Foreign Shorthair, is not new to Europe, the FIFE, or to England and the GCCF. Essentially this cat conforms to Siamese type but the cat is self-colored. That is, it is a solid-colored cat with no point color contrast. There are many colors available to this breed including the basic ebony which corresponds to the Siamese seal point, the chestnut which corresponds to the chocolate point, the lavender which corresponds to the lilac point and the blue, cream and red. There are white Orientals which include the blue-eyed white and green-eyed white but not the odd-eyed white. There are also varieties of shaded, smoke, tabby and particolor. What does all this mean and were did it start?

In actuality, it started in England with those ladies who worked so hard to produce a chocolate brown cat that was self-colored—solid in color with no markings. This cat, as we know, was called the Havana, then the Chestnut Foreign Brown and then the Havana again. It had come about with crosses between the chocolate point Siamese and either a black Domestic or a Russian blue. From these breedings came the Havana and also a lavender cat that was to become the Foreign lavender and was indeed a self-lilac. We must remember that the Havana and the Foreign lavender of England are both Oriental (Siamese) in type. Our Havana Brown is not of the same type and is not the same breed. In short, these foreign type cats in Europe and the two recognized in England to date are Oriental in type—they have a type like the Siamese with a solid colored body. FIFE has accepted the Foreign Shorthairs which are a counterpart of our Oriental Shorthairs. GCCF in England has accepted the Foreign lavender and the Havana but are not accepting the Foreign white because of their strict breeding regulations requiring four generations of like to like breeding. This latter requirement has hindered breeding these cats to the specifications that the breeders desire. So, in England each cat is treated as a separate breed and in Europe all self-colored Siamese type cats are grouped under the term Foreign Shorthairs.

In the United States, all self-colored Siamese type cats come under the term Oriental Shorthair. We also have our own Havana Brown breed which is a totally different breed. It is the hope and wish of all Oriental breeders here, and those breeding Foreign Shorthairs abroad, to have all these cats accepted under the name Oriental Shorthair and judged in the same class. These cats are obviously hybrids, as the Havana was a hybrid in the beginning. It was deliberately created by people looking to produce the type of cat they had envisioned or seen. Hybrid breeding produced this cat and is still used to further improve the breed. This creates fewer problems in Europe and our country than it has in England.

There are many people who, through the years, worked to make this breed possible, beginning with those women like Mrs. Hargreaves, Baroness von Ullman, Mrs. Elsie Fisher and Mrs. Munro-Smith, who worked with the Havana. In England those working with the whites include Pat Turner who works also with Havanas, Lavenders and Ebonies. Others in this country are numerous but interest has so increased in this past decade that the breed has been recognized by several associations for show or registration. The first Oriental Shorthairs in this country came from England and Holland. Again, what is needed now by the breeders is a universal way of naming and classifying these cats. CFF in May of 1976 allowed them for show and CFA has accepted them for provisional status. In October of 1976 CFA voted to accept this breed for championship status effective May 2, 1977.

Genetically, it has been found that this breed will breed true after several generations, then the problem of setting type and color becomes the important factor. What the breeders want are the Oriental colors and the extreme type of the Siamese. Breeding Oriental to Oriental can be done since there is a good variety of colors available already, thanks to breeding here and overseas. Breeding back to the American shorthair for color is feasible but not recommended as type is lost. For extreme type crosses are

Petmark Gany Kelea of Patapaw, a lavender male owned by Marilyn T. Buchanan. The breeders were Peter and Vicky Markstein. Photo by Ben Craven.

made back to good typey Siamese instead. Deep vivid green eye color is mandatory, only Siamese and Orientals with good eye color should be used. At the present the author finds the following crosses are acceptable for registration as Oriental Shorthair:

Siamese/colorpoint/lynxpoint to Oriental
Siamese/colorpoint/lynxpoint to American Shorthair
American Shorthair to Oriental
Oriental to Oriental

As pets the Oriental Shorthairs are like the Siamese in a way—playful and agile. However, the voice is softer than the Siamese. They have good stamina, good disposition and this new man-made breed with its Oriental look makes an exotic addition to any home.

The look of this cat is that of a svelte creature with long tapering lines. The head is a long, tapering wedge medium in size in good proportion to the body. The total wedge starts at the nose and flares out in straight lines to the tips of the ears forming a triangle, with no break at the whiskers. No less than a width of an eye

Tintadel's Lancelot Du Lilac, a lavender male owned and bred by Erica Mueller.

should be between the eyes. The skull is flat, there is no dip in the nose and no curves to the face. The nose is long and straight with no break. The muzzle is wedge-shaped and fine, the chin and jaw are medium in size—not massive nor receding. The ears are strikingly large, pointed, wide at the base and continuing the lines of the wedge. The almond shaped eyes are medium in size. They slant toward the nose in harmony with the lines of the wedge and the ears. The long, svelte body is medium in size, a combination of fine bones and firm muscles. Shoulders and hips continue the same sleek lines of a tubular body. The hips are never wider than the shoulders. The abdomen should be tight. The neck is long and slender, as are the legs, with the hind legs higher than the front. The paws are dainty, small and oval. The tail is long, thin at the base, tapering to a fine point at the tip. The coat is short, fine-textured, glossy and lays close to the body. The eye color is green but amber is permitted and in white cats either blue or green but not odd-eyed.

This cat is accepted in the following colors: white, ebony, blue, chestnut, lavender, red, cream, silver, cameo, ebony smoke, blue smoke, chestnut smoke, lavender smoke, cameo smoke and in the classic and mackerel tabby pattern the ebony, blue, chestnut, lavender, red, cream, silver and cameo. In these colors they are also accepted in the spotted tabby and ticked tabby pattern. In additon the tortoiseshell, blue-cream, chestnut tortie and lavender cream are accepted colors.

Grand Champion Willow Lane Precious, a cream Persian male, owned and bred by Isabel Roberts. Photo by Larry Levy.

Persian

The history of the Longhair in this country and in Europe is essentially the history of the Persian. In whatever way it came to us, it was accepted gratefully first by the English and then by the Americans as they imported this lovely breed. The Persian, once found and adopted, was improved upon with breeding programs in England both for type and color, and they went straight to the top of the show scene in short order. In America again they took the show scene and for years other breeds were hard put to compete. And today the Persian still commands an easy win—this beauty with a pretty face. If cats are to be exotic and elegant, this breed answers that demand. Where did the Longhair come from? Is the Persian a descendant of the Angora, or a mixture of that Longhair and a breed that was actually an early Persian?

I would prefer to think that the Persian is a natural breed and that massive surgery did not take place to turn the early Angora into the Persian of today. Evidence points to the fact that these two Longhairs did roam the world at approximately the same time and did breed together and we already know that such breeding caused the loss of the Angora as a breed for some years. If the two breeds did mix, something of each may have passed to the other. Having seen early pictures of the Persian it is not hard to believe that early writers and investigators found it hard to decide how they differed and it is equally obvious that the early Persian is a far cry from what we see in the show ring today.

It is believed that the Longhair came from Angora and from Persia—the latter being the home of the Persian. The King of Persia had his cat as did the King of Siam. The Persian cats went into Italy, France, England and other countries too. Longhairs generally have been known to have existed for some 300 years. They were noted in Italy during the Renaissance, and the Angoras in the

Gr. Ch. Khampur Corinthian of Char-O, a blue male, owned by Steve and Charmayne Davis. Breeders were Dr. and Mrs. Greer.

Angora section were not like the Persian. The Angora, for clarification, had a narrow head, tall ears, was more slender, and had a soft, silky fine fur while the Persian had a broad round head, smaller ears, a shorter body and a woolly, plushy coat. It is said they originated in Western Asia, in China, Burma, Afganistan, Persia and Russia. Whatever route the Persian took, it came to Italy, was prized in India, mixed with the Angora, gained interest from the breeders in England and became an established breed. What England started, America has finished with some beautiful specimens. This work was indeed lengthy, and select breeding programs went on for years since the first Persians were not typey at all as we know them today. They did have tall ears, long noses, were long in the body and higher on their legs, but the bone structure was not as heavy. Judging our pets from our breeders' show quality specimens we are going away from the old Persian toward the new. It is not easy since the tendency seems to be for the type to revert when careful breeding is not done. The show Persian today does not have to be extreme—this is not what the breeder is really looking for. As with all other breeds described in this book the word "balance" is the important key. The Persian who takes wins today is typey but in proportion and the type is not limited to the face but encompasses the entire body. The English started this process and worked wonders with color and type, but they still prefer a Persian with the older type more so than we do here in the US. Wherever the Persian came from, it is a certainty where it is going and that is to the top of the show circuit as long as the breed continues to develop as it has in the past. What could be more beautiful than the show Persian with its short body, its stocky legs and thick bones, its sweet rounded face with tiny ears and a good

Double Gr. Ch. Woodkiff Goldpiece of Char-O, a cream male, owned by Steve and Charmagne Davis. Breeder was Mrs. Thomas Gesel.

break that does not distort the face but rather shows an animal of quality? This cat is from head to tail in proportion and carries a healthy flowing coat.

The Persian as a pet is more docile and quiet than any shorthair and also more than a lot of Longhairs. Its playfulness as a kitten cannot be compared with other breeds for constant motion, mischievousness and the like. The Persian usually likes to be with you, but it can also be aloof. It seems to know the regal appearance it makes and just likes to sit around and look great. They can be found sprawled around in awkward positions with perfect ease. The cat will come to you for affection and as an adult is usually not demanding, but there are exceptions in all breeds. Its voice is quiet, varying in tone with its demands—food, sex, attention or just talking. To own a Persian is to have a companion that will likely sleep wherever you are working, waking to move when you do, then promptly resuming his rest after you have relocated. Or, the cat can go off and sleep for hours awakening only for dinner call. You may find the females, as with all breeds, more demanding and more pushy, but the males are usually a hunk of love that intrudes into your daily pace in a more subtle manner. They don't usually wrap themselves around your neck or nuzzle, but they are simply there and even the largest stud male can be gentle and loving. Whether a male or a female they are a joy to own. Even a ten year old will play like a kitten if the mood strikes. However, such play is modified: a piece of paper will be sniffed, pushed lightly and cautiously, batted with great energy for a few seconds, then forgotten. I do not find my Persians performing many stunts using their paws, balancing on awkward places or climbing with any great frequency. They find a sunny spot and sleep. But, for sheer beauty the Persian is my own love and I admit to prejudice here. There is nothing lovlier than a well-groomed Persian regally sitting in the doorway to greet guests as they arrive. Such a cat is hard to ignore!

Describing the Persian is hard to do as many breeders see a different type cat than do others. Some like the small face with the extreme type, others like a large cat, some prefer them very small and very cobby. However, the Persian has a standard and judges must be governed by that standard allowing for interpretation and for the final judgement between two cats that are equally good but

Linda Darville's Dar-Lin's Golden Topaz, a chinchilla golden female.

which have a different "look."

The Persian head should be round and massive, the emphasis here being on round as it will be throughout the standard. The Persian is a cat of gently curving lines that create a subtle rounded look. As with all breeds, it is imperative that it overpowers another part. Head type should never make for a winning cat if the body and other aspects are not the same quality, nor should any other aspect of the cat take precedence. It is the total cat that is judged and in the Persian the total cat has a rounded, solid, pretty look—an animal with good bone that flows gently from head to tail in perfect proportion. The skull of the Persian has a great breadth and the face is round with the bone structure being round also. There should be no tendency toward a head that shows any sign of a wedge or straight lines. Fur should never hide these features either—when the fur is pulled back the true shape of the head is there to see and it should be round in all aspects. The head itself is set on a short, thick neck, and this is very important. A Persian with a long chicken neck and fine bones that can be felt through the skin is not a good specimen. There should be a flow from the head to the shoulders with the neck being very short and very strong. It should not be obvious but should flow into the body.

The ears are small, with rounded tips and not unduly open at the base; they are tilted forward and set far apart. They should be low on the head, fitting into the rounded contour of the head. Tall, obvious ears that are wide open and set close together giving a different look to the cat is a poor aspect in a Persian. The ears should continue the round effect. The eyes, too, are round, large and full; they are set far apart and the color should be brilliant. They give a sweet expression to the face if they are truly round. Eyes of any other shape are wrong as are biased eyes that slant in any direction. The nose should be extremely short and broad with a definite stop where the nose meets the forehead. It should not be a break that totally submerges the cat's nose into its head so that it cannot breathe normally and the nose should not be narrow and long without a break. Both are poor examples of Persian—the former being too extreme, the latter not being typey enough. The cheeks on this cat should be full and the jaw should be broad and strong. However, the chin should be so strong that it protrudes past the upper lip. The teeth, in general, should match and that is entirely possible even with a good strong chin and jaw. The cat's body is cobby which means that it is short, low on the legs, deep in the chest, equally massive across the shoulders and the rump with a short, well-rounded middle section. It should be medium or large in size and all these aspects should be in proportion. Tall legs on a cobby body throw off such proportions—all aspects should be in harmony and in proportion. The cat should basically have a square build with a level back and short, thick, strong legs. The forelegs should be straight. The paws large, round and firm.

Above all, the bone on this cat should be thick and strong. Any feeling of slight bone or light weight either reflects poor breeding or in the case of weight alone, poor diet. The cat should feel substantial. The tail should be short but in proportion to the body and it should be carried without a curve, at an angle lower than the back. Cats tend to throw their tails about but a show Persian

Gr. Ch. Charoe's Muffin Man, a cream male. Bred and owned by Mrs. Roe Alexander. Photo by Curtis.

should stand with his tail in the proper position and above all should not carry it like a flag. The coat is long, thick and stands off from the body; it is of fine texture, glossy, full of life, and long all over the body, including the shoulders. The ruff should be immense and continue down between the front legs in a deep frill. The tail is full and the ear and toe tufts should be long.

The Persian is accepted for the following colors: blue-eyed white, copper-eyed white, odd-eyed white, blue, black, red, cream, chinchilla and shaded silver, blue smoke, black smoke, and cameo smoke, shell cameo and shaded cameo. It is accepted in the tortoiseshell, calico, dilute calico, blue-cream, bi-color, peke face red, peke face red tabby and tabbies in both classic and mackerel pattern in the following colors: blue, brown, silver, red, cream and cameo.

Above: The three accepted patterns of Ragdolls: the Mitted, Particolor and Colorpoint.
Below: Ragdoll kittens. These Ragdolls also appear in color on pages 76 and 292.

Ragdoll

The Ragdoll was originated about 10 years ago by Ann Baker who trademarked her cats with a franchise agreement concerning their breeding, showing, placement and continuation of the lines. Her standard was accepted by NCFA and these cats were crested to show them as true Ragdolls. The name was chosen and recognized in 1965. The cat was so named because of its ability to relax like a ragdoll.

The Ragdolls seem to have originated with a blue-eyed white female named Josephine. Offspring stem from Tiki, Fugianna and Daddy War Bucks—all children of the original mother. Ragdoll kittens are born white and do not obtain full color until two years of age. They reach full maturity at about three years of age. Males average about 15 to 20 pounds at maturity and females about five pounds less. They are about 18 inches high and have a 36-inch leg span. Above all, they resemble a beanbag, or a mink stole, or a ragdoll.

To date they are registered with ACA, ACFA, Crown, CFF, UCF and NCFA, though the standard differs due to the fact that a new faction has grown out of the original cats as sold by Ann Baker. NCFA accepts the cat only in the mitted form but other associations are accepting them in three color patterns: bi-color, colorpoint and mitted. This author does not wish to get into any controversy over how this happened or why, but does feel the breed should be included and so the standard will be a general one.

The cat itself is known for its hugeness, its thick fur, and its immunity or high tolerance to pain. They seem to lack fear or self-preservation instincts and have non-matting fur. They are also known for their limpness when being handled.

As pets they are a rave. They resemble, as stated a ragdoll or mink stole and will go limp in your arms when picked up. In fact, it is claimed they can be picked up without being awakened and can even be shaken without awakening them. They love to be mauled, are intelligent, will walk on a leash but love to be carried. They will not fight, say their owners, do not feel pain, but are affectionate and love to play. They are placid, calm, quiet. They adjust well to other animals but if they are afraid at all they will hide or crouch but not fight. It is like having a real live baby; they are easy to raise and have quiet tiny voices.

The Ragdoll has a head broad betwen the eyes and ears; the forehead slopes gradually down to a rounded chin. The male's head is wider than the female's. There is a flat spot on top of the head, about the middle of the head between the ears and extending towards the eyes a short distance. The nose is medium in length with a gentle break between the eyes. The cheeks are well developed, the whiskers are long and the chin well developed with a medium jaw. The neck is short, strong and heavy set. The breast bone should be expanded with a fluffy ruff that is full over it. The ears are medium in length, set high on the head with a slight tilt toward forward and broad at the base with a slightly rounded tip. The eyes are large and round and never crossed. The eyelid has a slight upward tilt at the outer edge. The body has an extremely heavy hind section and large loose muscles on the underside of the stomach. The male is huskier than the female. Males at maturity are very long from nose tip to the tip of the tail. The tail is long and full and proportionate to the body length. The legs are long and heavy with the back legs longer than the front. The coat is thick and soft, like rabbit fur; it is medium long to long. As stated the cat is accepted in at least one association only in the mitted cat, while other associations accept a bi-color, mitted or colorpoint Ragdoll in chocolate, seal, lilac and blue.

Overleaf:

Above, left: *Virgo's Fon-Fon, a seal point Balinese female, owned by Armen Boudakian and bred by Patricia Horton.*

Above, right: *Grand Champion Kamara Pussy Galore, a seal point Siamese female, owned and bred by Mr. and Mrs. Carl Boudreau. Photo by Pet Portraits.*

Below, left: *Virgo's Monti Rock IV, a male seal point Balinese, owned by Joyce Miller and bred by Patricia Horton.*

Below, right: *Grand Champion Kamara Hurry for Hazel, a chocolate point Siamese female, owned and bred by Mr. and Mrs. Carl Boudreau. Photo by Pet Portraits.*

Overleaf:

Above: *Torio Kismet, a blue eyed white Turkish Angora owned and bred by Mr. and Mrs. Thomas Torio. Photo by Larry Levy.*

Below: *Double Grand and Triple Champion Couer De Lion's Sisie of Mor-Ace, a stumpy Manx, owned by Anthony Morace and bred by Robert Ford, Jr. Photo by Kevin T. Sullivan.*

Champion Trafalgar's Baron Dunkirk of K-La, a cream British Shorthair, owned by Mr. and Mrs. Ed Rohrer and bred by Joel Presser. Photo by Larry Levy.

Overleaf:

Above, left: *Beachmor Joshua, a Scottish Fold owned and bred by Mr. and Mrs. F.M. Dreifuss.*

Above, right: *Mr. and Mrs. F.J. Dreifuss' calico Scottish Fold, Wyola Julliette of Beachmor. Both photos by Florence M. Harrison.*

Below, left: *Grand Champion Saramay Solikely of Overland, a white British Shorthair, owned by Bettijane Myjak and bred by Sara Meakin.*

Below, right: *Champion Taquin de St. Pierre, a Chartreux owned by Helen Gamon and bred by Madame S. Bastide. Photo by Tony Francis.*

Overleaf:

Above: *Grand Champion Namekagon Drucilla of Marcus, a Havana Brown, owned by Mark Hammon and bred by Velta Dickson. Photo by H & H.*

Below: *Grand Champion Jest-O-Mister O, a red Abyssinian male, owned and bred by Mr. and Mrs. Jack Ours. Photo by J'sen's.*

Overleaf:

Above: *Grand Champion Chataire's Chirawan, a Korat, owned by Mr. and Mrs. Jack Ours and bred by James Porter. Photo by George Brown.*

Below: *Bryric Trick or Treat, a calico Scottish Fold female, owned and bred by Karen A. Votava. Photo by Pete Miller.*

Overleaf:

Beachmor Jessica, a Scottish Fold, owned and bred by Mr. and Mrs. F.M. Dreifuss. Photo by Florence M. Harrison.

Overleaf:

Above, left: *International and Triple Champion No Ruz Sultan, an odd eyed white Turkish Angora male, owned and bred by Elaine Gesel.*

Above, right: *Shamba Letu's Pitti-Sing Mi-Ke, a female Japanese Bobtail, owned by Mr. and Mrs. Edward Skeels and bred by Carolyn McLaughlin. Photo by Floyd Gardner.*

Below: *Erica Mueller's cream Oriental Shorthair male, Scintilla Tangent of Tintadel.*

Overleaf:

Above: *Willowglen's Nadia, left, and Willowglen's Anastasia, champagne female Burmese kittens, owned and bred by Caroly L. Osier. Photo by Jim Cooper.*

Below: *Isabel Roberts' blue female Persian, Willow Lane Mistletoe, a Grand Champion. Photo by Larry Levy.*

Overleaf:

Above: *Mi-Ho's Haiku, a tortie female Japanese Bobtail, owned and bred by Barbara Hodits.*

Below: *A tortie female Japanese Bobtail, Mi-Ho's Mikeneko, owned and bred by Barbara Hodits. Photos by Michael J. Hodits.*

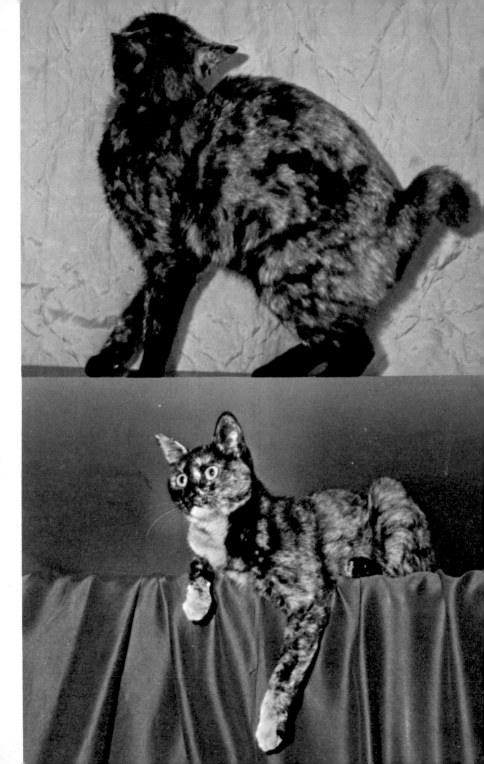

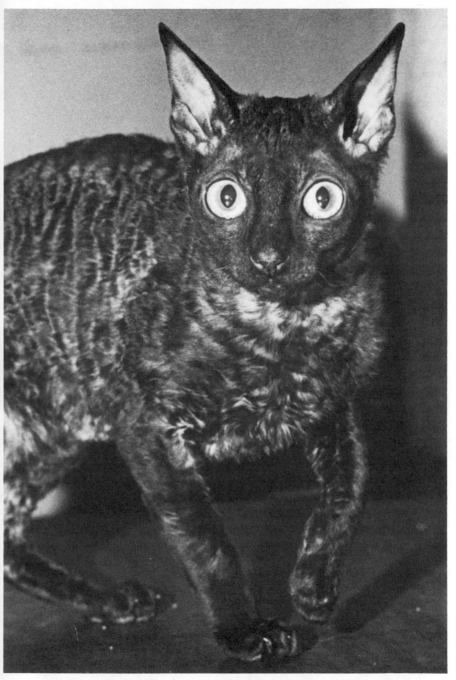

Gunter Grobe's Champion Katzenberg's Hatsheput, a black smoke cornish Rex female. Breeder was Ingeborg Urcia. Photo by Harriet Oswald.

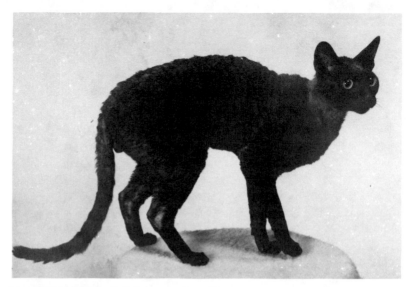

Above: Gr. Ch. Kurli-Q Satan's Dark Shadow, a black male Rex, owned by Bernadette A. Madden.
Below: Gr. Ch. Bien-Fur Flash of Innisfree, a blue female, owned by Erica Mueller.

Rex

The Rex is a case of spontaneous mutation discovered for the first time in 1950 in Bodmin Moor, Cornwall, England in a litter born to a tortie and white domestic Shorthair mother and a ginger-colored male—both normally coated. The sire and dam were farm cats owned by Mrs. Nina Ennismore who also had bred rabbits and was familiar with the first recorded Rex rabbit, the Castorrex. To get such a mutation both parents must carry the Rex gene or it must be an original mutation, practically an act of God. This first Rex was called Kallibunker and was known as the English Rex or the Cornish Rex since there was later to be a second strain of English Rex. Mrs. Ennismore, on the advice of geneticist Jude and Stirling-Webb mated this cat to his mother and produced a male Rex named Poldhu.

The next Rex cat seems to have been born in 1953 in Ohio when Miss Mary Hedderman produced Toni from a normal coated domestic litter. Then in Germany there came word that a black curly female had been taken in by a Dr. Scheuer-Karpin. Her name was Lammchen and with her son in 1957, named Fridolin, produced Sputnik. In 1960 Mrs. Muckenhaupt's son was in East Berlin and went to see Dr. Scheuer-Karpin. He brought back two females, one from Lammachen, the other from her daughter Curlee. Marigold and Jet, as they were called, were born in 1960. Then Christopher, the first curly German Rex, was sent to Mrs. Joan O'Shea in 1961. These ladies were early pioneers of the Rex and even today Mrs. Muckenlaupt can be seen at local shows here in the East showing her beautiful Rex.

In the spring of 1957 Mrs. Frances Blancheri from California imported a blue female Rex, Lamorna Cove, from Mrs. Ennismore and a red tabby male kitten called Pendennis Castle. The female had been bred to Poldhu, her father, before being shipped.

Grand and International Champion Rumplesilkskin Tam, a parti-color brown and white tabby Rex, owned by Mr. and Mrs. George Q. Thornton. Breeder was Margaret Slocum. Photo by Rick Barnes.

A litter was born containing two blue and white kittens—Diamond Lil of Fan-T-Cee who was to be owned by Mrs. Peggy Galvin and Marmaduke of Dazzling to be owned by Mrs. Helen Weiss. They are behind the English strain here in this country. A mutation occured in Oregon, in 1959, reported by Mrs. Mildred Stringham of Oregon who found a little black and white curly kitten in a normal litter. This kitten was named Kinky Marcella.

Then in 1960 back in England the second strain of English Rex appeared. Miss Beryl Cox of Buckfastleigh, Devon, had a curly-coated cat registered by her as Kirlee; it was a black male. Brian stirling-Webb purchased the cat which he bred to a Rex queen from the first English strain and produced all normal-coated cats, thus the two strains were not the same. This strain became the Devon strain (Gene II) while the first strain was the Cornish strain (Gene I). In all countries but the United States two strains of Rex are recognized—Devon and Cornish—but here one standard reflects a combination of only the German and the Cornish. Canada is the exception as they recognize the Devon strain.

Twenty years after the appearance of the first Rex it was proved by breeders working together in this country that the German and Cornish Rex mutations are genetically the same and can be used together to produce Rex kittens. One of the first crosses known to have been made was by Bob and Dell Smith of Rodell Cattery and Charles and Mabel Tracy of Paw Print Cattery. The Smiths sent a Cornish male called Rodell's Rimsky to be mated to the Tracy's German female Rex, Paw Prints Schatz. The litter produced Rex kittens. Such is not the case with the Devon Rex which will produce all normal-haired cats when bred to the Cornish Rex. In the United States UCF was the first to accept the Rex and this stan-

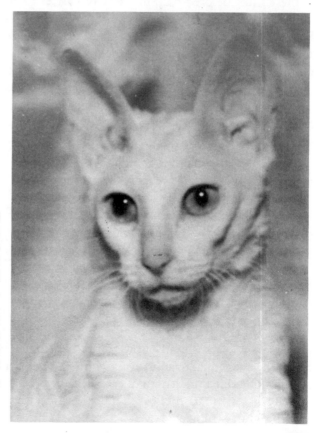

Grand Champion and Premier Rindy's Haven Nipper of Van Dol, an odd eyed white, owned by Mr. and Mrs. Virgil Nitz. Breeders were Ed and Harriet Rindfleisch.

dard was written by Peggy Galvin and Ann Manley using Diamond Lil as an example—she being out of Cornish lines.

Genetically such a mutation is fascinating. The coat of the Rex is unlike any other cat's coat and perhaps only the Wirehair or the Sphynx can command such attention. It has been determined that Rex do not resemble their parent breed and both parents must carry the Rex gene to have a Rex kitten appear in the litter. Thus the gene is recessive. When two Rex of the same strain are mated the result is 100% Rex coated kittens. It has been determined that the Cornish, German and Oregon Rex are similar in hair type. The Devon Rex has a different type of hair and few whiskers. The Cornish and German Rex are genetically the same. Since the Rex gene is recessive when bred to normal-coated domestics a Rex will produce all normal-coated kittens carrying the Rex gene and one of these must be bred back to a Rex or carrier to get Rex kittens.

The Rex Breeders United was formed in 1969 and is CFA affiliated, publishes the *Forum* four times a year. The Rex Society International, unaffiliated, works for the interest of the Rex. This group came into being in 1962 to bring breeders together and promote the breed. The German Rex Society was organized in 1967. The Rex Breeders United has done much to unite those with different strains of Rex and to work together and publish their findings.

The Rex as a pet is individualistic, playful, affectionate and has a high degree of curiosity and intelligence. It is a spirited cat and will not tolerate being treated badly. It is gentle and seldom uses its small voice. It makes a loving companion and is a real lap cat but is also active and agile. It learns quickly, loves to please and is people oriented.

The Rex has a small, narrow head that is about one-third again as long as the width and has a definite whisker break. The muzzle narrows slightly to a rounded end. The ears are large, wide at the base and come to a modified point at the top; they are placed high on the head and are held erect. The eyes are medium in size, oval in shape and slant slightly upward. There should be a space between the eyes equal to a full eye's width. The nose is Roman with a length one-third the length of the head. In profile it is a straight line but has a squarish effect. The cheeks are lean and muscular and the chin strong and well-developed. The body is small to medium and the torso long and slender. The back is arched with the lower line of the body following the upward curve. The shoulders are well-knit and the rump rounded and well-muscled. The legs are long and slender. The hips are well-muscled, somewhat heavy in proportion to the rest of the body. The Rex stands high on its legs and has dainty, slightly oval paws. The tail is long, slender and tapering to an end and is extremely flexible. In general, it is fine-boned and delicate; its agility and fast movements aided by its legs and build. The coat on this cat is short, extremely soft, silky and completely free of guard hairs. It is relatively dense; a tight, uniform marcel wave, lying close to the body and extending from the top of the head across the back, sides and hips continuing to the tip of the tail characterizes the Rex coat. The fur on the underside of the chin and on the chest and abdomen is short and noticeably wavy. Under the coat, it is a firm and muscular cat.

The Rex is accepted in the following colors: blue-eyed white, copper-eyed white, odd-eyed white, black, blue, red, cream, chinchilla, shaded silver, black smoke, blue smoke, classic and mackerel tabby; silver, red, brown, blue, cream; tortoiseshell, calico, dilute calico, blue-cream, bi-color and other Rex colors.

Champion Lov'N Blu's Carefree Carley, a Russian Blue female, owned and bred by Dr. and Mrs. Robert G. Sigler.

Russian Blue

As illustrated in discussions of previous breeds, the blue cat has appeared in history for centuries. This color is a mutation from the black, but once blue has been achieved blue to blue will breed true. There are many varieties of blue cats but the shade of blue is not the same and the type and coat texture vary greatly.

In the late 1800's there was noticed a particular blue cat with a silvery blue coat which was plush, dense, and with a short double coat. These were believed to have originated in Russia in a place called Archangel and thus they came to be called the Archangel cats or Archangel blues. It is believed that the cats were trapped in northern Russia for their beautiful coats and that this coat served as protection against the climate of this semi-arctic area of northern Russia. Their coat provided insulation as the outer coat had longer guard hairs to provide protection and to repel water while the short downy undercoat kept the body warm. The cats left this Russian northern port and came to England and to Sweden by way of the Vikings.

In 1880 the first Russian Blue was shown in England. Two breeders showed an interest in the breed. Mrs. Carew-Cox owned two of them called Yula and Bayard that were imported around 1900 from Archangel. Later Miss Marie Rochford would make the name of "Dunloe" famous all over the world with her Russian Blues. In the late 1880's when they first came to be known in England and shown, all Russian Blues were judged in the same class as all other shorthaired blues. Around 1912 two classes of blue were set up, the British Blue and the Blue Foreign of which the Russian was a part. The owners did not like this and did not consider the cat foreign in type and continued to call it Russian and finally in 1939 the name was changed back to Russian. Dates on the Russian in America vary and it is hard to pinpoint exactly

Champion Tsar Bli's Gingerella, owned and bred by Donna Fuller. Photo by John Turner.

when it was first shown and it is disputed whether the name was finally changed to Russian in the late 1930's or the early 1940's.

Reports too vary on the Russian Blue in America. Some say it was imported as early as 1888 and registered in 1900. Mrs. Clinton Locke around 1900 imported from England from a breeder named Mr. Towlerton Flansholm a cat named Lockehaven Royal Blue. Differences in registries undoubtedly account for discrepancies in dates. In the 1940s cats were exported from England by Marie Rochford of Dunloe Cattery. The cats were sent to Mr. C.A. Comhaire and were named Dunloe Jan and Dunloe Blue Silk.

This breed is a natural breed, its color and type being unique as well as its coat. It cannot be lumped with other blues such as the American Shorthair blue, the Korat, the Oriental blue or the British blue or Exotic Shorthair blue. Blues may at one time have been lumped together but now the standards show great differences in type, coat and in the shade and type of blue coat required. Again, this is believed to have been a natural breed from Russia.

Today, breeders say the best Russian Blues come from England and from Sweden. Actually, the best Russian Blues today are primarily Swedish lines mixed with moderate amounts of old English. Today's English Russian Blues are not of the same type

266

Grand Champion Tsar Blu's Dazzling Adonis, male, owned and bred by Donna Fuller. Photo by Heritage Studio.

as those bred in the U.S. The English require high ear set and in the United States that is a fault. It is another case of the English type of a breed being more foreign in type than that of the US and therefore English standards do not reflect American breeds.

Genetically, the blue cat bears little discussion. It breeds true. It is a recessive color, a mutation or dilution of the black which is a dominant color. Russian Blues should never be bred out to other breeds or they won't breed true for color or for type.

As pets they are quiet and tend to be individualistic. They have silvery voices which they use only when they have something to say, not just to hear themselves talk. They are gentle and shy but loyal to their owners. They have good senses and are fast and well coordinated and love to play. This is a cat that requires little care and is a loyal, lovely and graceful breed.

The head of this breed is broad across the eyes due to wide-set eyes and thick fur. The top of the skull is flat and long. The ears are rather large and wide at the base with the tips more pointed than rounded. The skin of the ears is thin and translucent with very little inside furnishing. The outside of the ear is scantily covered with short, very fine hair and leather usually showing through. The ears are set far apart, as much on the side as on the top of the head. The eyes are set wide apart too and rounded or

Donna Fuller's Grand Champion Tsar Blu's Fitzwilliam. Photo by John Turner.

A head study of Dr. and Mrs. Robert G. Sigler's Grand Champion Lov'N Blue's Silver Dew Drop.

oval in shape. The neck is long and slender, but appearing short due to the thick fur and high placement of the cat's shoulder blades. The nose is straight and medium in length without a break and the chin is level. The cat's body is fine-boned, long, lithe and graceful and the legs are long and fine-boned. The paws are small and slightly rounded. The tail is long and tapering from a moderately thick base. The coat is short, dense, fine and plush. The double coat stands out from the body due to the density and it is soft and silky to the feel. The color is an even bright blue throughout with no white anywhere. Lighter or lavender shades of blue are preferred. The guard hairs are silver-tipped giving the cat a silvery sheen or lustrous appearance. The nose leather is slate gray and the pads are lavender pink or mauve. The cat's eyes should be vivid green.

Bryric Daisy May, a female blue cream Scottish Fold, owned by Carol A. Bellicitti. Breeder was Karen Votava. Photo by Marcia L. Dressler.

Scottish Fold

The first Scottish Fold was a white female cat named Susie. She was seen by Mr. William Ross in a Perthshire farmyard in 1961. He realized how unique she was and asked the owner for a similar kitten if one was born. The first Fold, Susie, was a family pet of unknown origin with a pure white coat, short thick tail and ears that were folded down onto the head rather than standing up in normal position. In two years the Rosses, William and Mollie, received one of the two Folds born to Susie. Her name was Denisla Snooks. At maturity she was bred to a red tabby and the resulting litter contained one male Fold which the Rosses kept. Meanwhile, they had acquired a female British Shorthair named Lady May and they bred her to the first Fold male whose name was Snowball. The result was five Scottish Folds, among them Denisla Snowdrift, a white male. A further breeding between Snooks and a normal eared cat named Rylands Regal Gent produced Denisla Hester of Mini and Denisla Hector. These cats are the foundation stock of the new Scottish Fold breed and their progeny have passed to devoted breeders throughout the world. Among this group are Edward Grayson (Martina Cattery), Nan Simpson, Briony Sivewright, Patricia Turner, John Steele and Tony and Judith Hyde of Ackiltie Cattery and Neil Todd and Salle Wolf Peters of Wyola Cattery and Lyn Lamoureux.

Since the cat was first seen in 1961 breeding programs have begun. The cat was obviously a mutation—an act of God. Kittens in a litter may be normal (pricked) or folded.

Salle Wolf Peters was to become the first to breed the first registered Fold in this country. It is believed that Dr. Neil Todd worked with the Fold, as did others, but they did not become actively involved in promoting the cat in the fancy. One of the first imports was the above mentioned Denisla Hester of Mini who

Bryric Silver Bullion, a silver tabby male. Breeder-owner is Karen A. Votava. Photo by Pete Miller.

went to Lyn Lamoureux, who has written on the Fold in the US and in England. This cat of hers found its way to many breeders but was for a time leased to Salle Peters in 1972. She was bred to a black Exotic Shorthair called Leprechaun's Hurricane of Wyola and produced one Fold out of three kittens. The other two had normal ears. The first fold was called Wyola Jed Callant and was the first Fold registered in CFA, bred by a registered breeder and the first Fold shown in CFA. At the same time it is possible that Dr. Todd had been breeding Folds but these, it is believed, were sold privately. It is also possible that Hester may have been shown in another association before this, but Mrs. Peters led the way in CFA with the help of Mollie Ross, Eddie Grayson and Judith Hyde. Wyola Jed Callant was one of the first cats listed, along with the first Fold (Susie), on the list to gain acceptance in CFA. Mrs. Peters also imported two other cats from outside the US which were Martina Scottsman of Wyola and Ackiltie Cream Charmer of Wyola.

In the US after 1974 Mrs. Salle Wolf Peters founded the international Scottish Fold Association; Willie and Mollie Ross, founders of the breed, are co-presidents. The club's goals are to provide information, protect the welfare and promote the acceptance of the Scottish Fold as a breed for show competition. The I.S.F.A. Newsletter is published three times a year and membership information can be obtained from Mrs. Salle Peters, 664 Valerie Drive, Newton Square, PA 19073.

In October of 1974 the Cat Fanciers Association of Red Bank, N.J. met in executive session and voted to accept the Scottish Fold as a new mutation of nature and experimental registration in CFA

Two Scottish Folds owned by Joyce Warner. Left: Bryric Calico Girl of Cirrus, a calico female. Right: Bryric Silver Streak of Cirrus, a silver and white tabby. Breeder was Karen A. Votava.

is now open. After January 1, 1976 the Fold was accepted for registration, with the specification that the only hybridization would be with the American Shorthairs. In England, the British Shorthair is used as an outcross exclusively. As of May 1977 the Board of Directors of the Cat Fanciers Association approved the advance of this breed from experimental to provisional status.

The breeding of the Fold seems to be based on the theory of breeding a Scottish Fold cat (the best you can find) to a prick-eared cat of the best possible health, type and temperament. Such a cat can be found in the British Shorthair in England and in the American Shorthair in America or among the prick-ear offspring of Folds. When Folds are mated to prick-ear cats you will have fifty percent Fold offspring and fifty percent prick-ear offspring. The prick-ears are valuable in your breeding program but they do not carry the Fold gene and cannot produce Fold kittens unless mated to a Fold.

The personality of the Fold is terrific and it makes a good pet. It loves to win friends and is gentle, sweet and sensible. It seems

Wyola Jed Callant, owned and bred by Salle Wolf Peters. He was the first Scottish Fold registered and shown in the U.S.

Martina Scottman of Wyola (Imp), owned by Salle Wolf Peters. Breeder was Eddie Grayson.

always the optimist and is excellent with other cats, children, strangers, and loved ones.

The Scottish Fold has a massive round head, well set on a short, thick neck. There is considerable breadth between the ears. The ears are distinguished by a definite fold line. The degree of fold will vary from a small, tightly folded ear to a somewhat larger, less tightly folded ear. The ear is usually small and folded forward and down at the top of the ear pocket. Kittens may have a slight fold but in the mature cat a definite fold line should be visible. The nose is short, broad and with a gentle break or indentation. The cheeks are full and rounded with a full, well developed chin and broad jaw. The eyes are round, large and full, well opened; eye color will be related to color. The body is short, cobby, broad across the shoulders and across the rump; it should be powerful and well knit, compact and well balanced. The chest is full and broad. Its tail is less flexible than that of other cats and thick at the base. It is either short with a rounded extremity or longer and tapering slightly. The coat should be thick, dense, soft in texture and short.

The Scottish Fold is accepted in the following colors: white, black, blue, red, cream, chinchilla, shaded silver, shaded cameo, shell cameo, black smoke, blue smoke, cameo smoke, classic tabby and mackerel tabby pattern in silver, red, brown, blue, cream and cameo; tortoiseshell, calico, dilute calico, blue-cream and bi-color.

Champion JoRene Dumbo, a lilac point Siamese, owned and bred by Dr. Irene B. Horowitz.

Siamese

The history of the Siamese is as difficult to trace as that of the Persian since it dates back in history and reports are conflicting depending on the association in question or the source of reference. Just when the Siamese came to the cat fancy is not known exactly nor is it known exactly what the original cat of Siam looked like. There are varying descriptions that have come to us. Some say it was a dun colored cat with dark, chocolate points, others say it was light gray with black points and others insist it was a solid colored cat—a seal colored cat—that was probably brown. It is possible that all varieties did occur in Siam, or Thailand as it is known today. We have stated that the Korat is from Thailand and considered the people's cat, rather than the Siamese cat which was supposed to have been the favored cat of the King and priests. In addition there is the Burmese, which is also supposed to be from Siam originally and considered along with the other two as good luck bringers. So, solid colored cats may have been seen and various shades of color points and body color are possible. Obviously, the work of English breeders perfected what came to them and gave us the distinct colors we have today.

History says that the Siamese was indeed revered by the priests and the King and lived in the Royal Palace and was considered the Royal Cat of Siam. They guarded the palace and actually worked, according to some reports. They were seen too in the Buddhist temples and were believed to be guardians there and used in religious ceremonies. It does seem important to note that these special cats were small in number and that other Siamese type cats roamed the streets of Siam at will and were not considered special. In effect, there was a royal bloodline which was separate and apart from the domestic Siamese, if legend tells a true tale. It was said that a visitor would be told that the royal ones were not sold or given away lightly. They were given as special gifts or some might have been stolen from the palace and sold again, but that is speculation. The cats, which were considered royal, were perfect in that they were bred carefully and did not have crossed eyes, improper markings or kinked tails. The mongrel cats that roamed the streets were badly marked, had kinked tails, crossed eyes and bred freely with domestic cats. Thus it was obvious that the temple cats were bred with care and any ones with problems were not used again in the breeding program.

Some say the Siamese appeared in England in 1884. These two were supposed to have come with Mr. Owen Gould, but it is also reported the Siamese were first shown at the Crystal Palace in 1871 and at other shows. This appearance in 1871 is documented by the fact that the cats appeared in the show catalog. Since the first ones coming into England in 1884 were supposed to be from the King of Siam to the British Consul-General then perhaps

Grand Champion Kamara Valentino of Karyzam, a seal point male, owned by Rae and Dick McCarthy. Breeders were Carl and Marcia Boudreau. Photo by Pet Portraits.

Grand Champion Singa Blue Song, a blue point female, owned and bred by Jeanne Singer. Photo by Jane Howard.

these were true temple cats of good type and such may not have been the case with earlier Siamese. The first Siamese champion in England was a cat called Wankee imported from Hong Kong by Mrs. M. Robinson in 1896. In 1901 the Siamese Cat Club of England was established and the first standard was drawn up by the club in 1902. All these first Siamese were sealpoint, but an existing report states that a Mr. Spearman showed a bluepoint at the first show at Holland House in London in 1896, but even six years later in 1902, the color was still not accepted. In fact the judges could not decide what the cat was when shown by Mr. Spearman. Later each colorpoint was accepted in its turn but it took time.

In the United States, Siamese began coming in around the late 1800's, but the first recorded Siamese was that of Mrs. Rutherford B. Hayes in 1879. Mrs. Blanche Arral of New Jersey was said to have brought actual temple Siamese to this country as she was presented with a pair by the King of Siam. Two of the earliest Siamese to arrive and be recorded were Lockehaven Siam and Lockehaven Sally Ward, who belonged to Mrs. Clinton Locke of

Chicago. These cats were registered around 1900 and then Mrs. A.H. Hoag registered a neuter called Chone and later a cat called Madison California. Chone was the first neuter champion and was owned by Mary P. Freeman. He also was the first American bred Siamese. Madison California was the first whole Siamese to make champion that had been born in the US and Sally Ward was the first import to make champion. Another early exhibitor and breeder was Miss Jane Cathcart who imported her cats from France and England including famous champion Siam de Paris. The Siamese Cat Society of America was founded in 1909. Virginia Cobb saw her first Siamese at Madison Square Garden and began research into the genetics of the breed with Dr. Clyde E. Keeler, the geneticist from Harvard. Their studies are interesting not only in relation to the Siamese but also in the controversy over the Colorpoint Shorthair.

The English standard was modified and in 1927 a revised standard was drawn up and accepted in 1927 by CFA. The first Siamese specialty show was in 1928. Another revised standard was drawn up with the help of Virginia Cobb and the National Siamese Cat Club. Thanks to the research done by Cobb and Keeler the bluepoint was accepted as another color of Siamese.

The apple-headed Siamese that many people think of as the original Siamese with its thickset look was probably a cross between a Siamese and a domestic. However, the earliest true Siamese were small and dainty with marten-like pointed faces, large ears, and deep blue eyes, all of which gave the cat a rather delicate look. Today's standard Siamese follows this breed's natural tendency and is simply a "refined" version of the first Siamese.

As a pet the Siamese is alert, active, personable and dog-like. It has a banshee-like voice when in heat and can be persistent when it wants. They are prolific breeders probably because they are a natural breed. They are content to be alone but love to be with their owners. They are touchingly dependent and demonstrative with their owners for whom they hold great admiration. Life to them is a game and they love to learn tricks; they also love children and overall are very active. Their voice range is amazing with many different tones and different cries for every occasion. All in all the Siamese is very smart, agile, active, enchanting and above all, very Oriental in its beautiful features.

The Siamese has a long, tapering wedge-shaped head, medium in size. The total wedge should start at the nose and flare out in straight lines to the tips of the ears forming a triangle, with no break at the whiskers. No less than the width of an eye should mark the distance between the eyes. The skull is flat and there is no dip in the nose and no curves or bulges to the face. The ears are strikingly large, pointed, wide at the base, thus continuing the lines of the wedge. The eyes are almond shaped and medium in size. They slant towards the nose in harmony with the lines of the wedge and the ears and they should be uncrossed. The nose is long and straight with no break. The muzzle is fine and wedge-shaped and the chin and jaw medium in size, neither receding nor massive. The body is medium in size, dainty, long and svelte. It is a combination of fine bones and firm muscles. The shoulders and hips continue the same sleek lines of a tubular body. The abdomen is tight and the hips are never wider than the shoulders. The neck is long and slender as are the legs, with the hind legs higher than the front. The tail is long, thin and tapering to a fine point. The coat is short, fine-textured, glossy and lying close to the body. The color of the body is even with subtle shading when allowed. There must be a definite contrast between the body color and the point color. The points include the mask, ears, legs, feet and tail and should be dense, clearly defined and all of the same shade. The mask covers the entire face and is connected to the ear by tracings. The mask should not extend over the top of the head.

The Siamese is accepted in the following four colors: seal point, chocolate point, blue point and lilac point. In those countries and organizations that do not recognize the Colorprint Shorthair as a separate breed, these colors are all included in the Siamese breed.

Double Champion June's Dancing Moon, the first all-American Somali. This ruddy male is owned and bred by Mr. and Mrs. S. Negrycz. Photo by Alice Su.

Somali

Despite the exotic name, which is a tribute to the alleged African genesis of the Abyssinian, the Somali is as Canadian as the maple leaf. When longhaired kittens first started popping up in purebred Abyssinian litters ten or more years ago, Canada may have been the birthplace of some of the first Somalis. They also started to appear in the US and European championship Abyssinian bloodlines.

The cat has been described as looking like a "wild animal," a "soft orange cloud" and a "striking red fox." They are basically a medium to large sized cat, generally larger than the Aby shorthair. They have a full dense, fine-textured coat, and the tail is full also, with shorter length hair permitted over the cat's shoulders. The cat matures a little more slowly than its Abyssinian progenitors and the full color and ticking don't come till eighteen months. In its long silky coat, the ticked guard hairs mostly disappear and the tickings shift to the short hairs. The cat has the same distinguishing markings and personality as the Abyssinian.

The genetic origins of the Somali are not quite known. Debate still rages over what actually occurred. Some insist an Aby had been crossed with a Longhair but this is not the case; it is not a hybrid breed. More likely, it is a mutation as with the longhaired Manx and the Balinese. The basic type of the cat has not changed and neither has its color, but its coat length has. Therefore, in the case of this mutation the awn hair and down hair of the coat were somehow lengthened. The result is a longish, very soft, silky body coat with a plume-like tail. The longhair gene is recessive and elusive. The same breedings of a pair of Shorthairs that produce Somali kittens will have many more shorthairs before producing another Somali. However, because this gene is recessive the basic laws of genetics apply. Two Somalis bred together will breed true; they will produce Somali kittens. But, for Somali kittens to appear in a litter it is necessary for both parents to be Somalis or to carry the gene for Longhair.

Their status in the cat fancy began in the United States in 1972 when the Somali Cat Club of America was formed and the breed was accepted by NCFA and then ICF, Crown and CFF and by CCA in Canada. The club promotes recognition of the breed and its betterment. It also sends out a club newsletter on a regular basis and offers rosettes to any show where a Somali is entered. 1975 showed the Somali appearing in *Cats Magazine* in AA scoring. Progress towards acceptance has been steady and the breed has met with enthusiasm. The Somali, like the Aby, is known for its characteristic ticking but also for its distinct personality. It is amusing, entertaining, affectionate and alert. It is a very lively cat, intensely curious and intelligent. However, it is a quiet cat and rarely uses its voice.

This cat has a head that is a modified, slightly rounded wedge without any flat planes and the brow, cheek and profile lines all gently contoured. There is a slight rise from the bridge of the nose to the forehead and there should be width between the ears. The muzzle follows this gentle contour and the chin is full, not overshot or undershot, and has a rounded appearance. It should not be sharply pointed and there should be no look of foxiness or whisker break. The ears are large, alert and moderately pointed, broad and cupped at the base. The ear is set on a line towards the rear of the skull. The inner ear has horizontal tufts that reach nearly to the other side of the ear and tufts are desirable. The eyes are almond shaped, large, brilliant and expressive. They are accented by a dark lid skin, encircled by a light-colored area. Above each eye a short dark vertical pencil stroke with a dark pencil line goes from the upper lid toward the ear. The color preferred is a rich, deep gold or green. The body is medium long, lithe and graceful showing well-developed muscle strength. The rib cage is rounded and the back is slightly arched giving the appearance of a cat about to spring. When standing, the Somali gives the impression of being quick and on tip-toe looks very alert. The tail has a full brush and is thick at the base and slightly tapering. The ticking on this cat should begin at the skin with a ruddy tone alternating with black for ruddies or red alternating with chocolate brown for red

Champion L'Air De Rauch Rocky Raccoon of Foxtail, a ruddy male, owned by Patricia Nell Warren. Breeder is Mrs. M. Rauch. Photo by Manny Greenhaus.

Somalis. The coat texture is very soft to the touch, extremely fine-textured and double-coated; the denser the coat the better. The length is medium except over the shoulders where a slightly shorter length is permitted. Preference is given to a cat with a ruff and breeches giving a full coat look.

There are two colors, the ruddy and the red, which are described at the back of the book in the color section and which correspond to the required color in the Abyssinian.

Grand Champion Dutchie's Nefertiti of Mewsi-Kal, a black female Sphynx, shown with one foreleg raised in a stance characteristic of the breed. She is owned by Sandy Kaiser.

Sphynx

This is a spontaneous mutation that appeared in Ontario, Canada in 1966. In a litter born to a black and white housecat named Elizabeth, one cat was entirely hairless. A new breed was in the making but much work lay ahead, as this hairless cat is not easy to breed. Interest was taken by a Siamese breeder and a Mrs. Kees Tenhove of Canada. CFA gave the breed provisional status and then revoked it. Many original breeders stopped breeding this cat. Crown finally recognized them for championship competition in 1971 and to date only two have been shown. The first Sphynx champion was Dutchie's Nefertiti, shown by Mrs. Mardell Jones in 1972. The cat was then purchased by Sandy Kaiser in 1973 and she has been carrying on her breeding program since then. The cat has become a grand in Crown and Sandy believes she is the only breeder of this breed in this country and that in addition to her whole family there is only one other cat around and that is a spay in Florida. It is a shame as they are a unique breed. (Recently, Mrs. Kaiser sold two kittens to a Peter Gann of Iowa who will work with this breed.)

The Sphynx is a simple recessive. To get a hairless kitten you must breed a hairless to a hairless, a hairless to a carrier, or a carrier to a carrier. The kittens are born nude and gradually grow a little hair later. For outcrosses the domestic is used as that was the original parent. However, this mutation, as with the Rex, did not just change its hair length, it changed its type also. The Sphynx does not look like a domestic from which it came.

As a pet, Mrs. Kaiser says that the cat is a love, purrs loudly and incessantly. They are people-oriented, but don't like other cats. They also don't like to be held or cuddled but will sit or stand on your lap purring sometimes with one foreleg lifted. This is a common stance—one foreleg lifted. Never do they put their hairless bellies on a cold floor but prefer to lie on warm surfaces. They have a unique way of sitting with both hind legs under, hocks together and fanny off the ground.

Seeing the Sphynx is a unique experience and so is touching one. For one thing this is a breed with a high body temperature and they sweat. The head of the cat is slightly longer than it is wide and with a slight but definite whisker break. The profile has a stop at the bridge of the nose and another may be felt above the eyes. The neck is long, slender, giving a snakey appearance to the head. It is barrel-chested giving a bowed appearance to the legs. The body is medium long with a modified "tuck up" behind the ribs. The cat is hard and muscular and has a medium bone structure, it is not delicate. The tail is long, tapering from the body to the tip, and the length is in proportion to the body. The paws are oval, dainty and with long slender toes. This cat is not hairless, it is covered with a very short down that is almost invisible to the eye and touch. On the points (ears, muzzle, tail, feet and testicles) there will be short, tightly packed soft hair. No whiskers or eyebrows are to be seen. A very light dispersion down the spine of short, wiry hair is allowable. The cat is firm and muscular and warm to the touch, and its coat will feel like suede. This cat cannot be small, the male adult weighs a minimum of eight pounds and the female a minimum of seven pounds. The eye color is in keeping with the coat color except where green, gold or hazel eye color is acceptable in the black and white particolors. The coat color is accepted in all color and markings as for the Manx and Rex and the Domestic Shorthair.

Overleaf:

Champion Gelin of Torio, an amber eyed white female Turkish Angora, owned by Mr. and Mrs. Thomas Torio and bred at the Turkish Zoo in Ankara. Photo by Larry Levy.

Overleaf:

Above: *Three Ragdolls, left to right, the mitted, parti-color, and colorpoint. Photo courtesy of Laura Dayton.*

Below: *Master Grand and Double Grand Champion Tunxis Valley Nutmegger of Theta, a cream Persian owned by Mr. and Mrs. Bob Wilson and bred by Marianne I. Fischer. Photo by Chet Burak.*

Overleaf:

*Prunes Napolean of Bor-Al, a black male repre-
senting the unique Sphynx breed. He is owned by
Sandy Kaiser and was bred by The Bawas. Photo
by Mr. Deverman.*

Overleaf:

Mr. and Mrs. Carl Boudreau's lilac point female Siamese, Grand Champion Kamara Mysteria. Photo by Pet Portraits.

Overleaf:

Grand Champion Dixey's Priscilla, a silver tabby American Shorthair, owned by Mr. and Mrs. Joseph Anderson and bred by Diana Dixey.

Overleaf:

Above: *A red classic tabby Maine Coon, Champion Razzberi Ripple of Candilu, owned by Canda Beeler and Lucy Kwasiborski.*

Below: *Patricia Nell Warren's ruddy Somali male, Champion L'Air De Rauch Rocky Raccoon of Foxtail, bred by Mrs. M. Rauch. Photo by Manny Greenhaus.*

Overleaf:

Quadruple Grand Champion, International Quintuple and Quadruple Champion brown tabby Maine Coon male, Mor-Ace's Satan, owned and bred by Anthony Morace. Photo by Kevin T. Sullivan.

Overleaf:

Bryric Patchwork, a calico Scottish Fold female, owned and bred by Karen A. Votava. Photo by Pete Miller.

Overleaf:

Marilyn Buchanan's Patapaw Justa Foo-Lin, a tortoiseshell Oriental Shorthair female. Photo by Ben Craven.

Sandy Kaiser's Grand Champion Sphynx, Dutchie's Nefertiti of Mewsi-Kal.

Two of Madalyn Dakin's natural mink Tonkinese. Above: Ch. Ulyssis of Madalyn, male. Photo by John Cowhey. Below: Ch. Dawn of Madalyn, female. Photo by Ken McKee. Both cats were bred by Dorothy Kelleher.

Tonkinese

The Tonkinese is a relatively new breed making great strides thanks to the devoted work of those trying to develop the breed. They are a new hybrid breed, produced by crossing two already established breeds: Siamese and a Burmese. The color of Siamese used can determine differences in the color of Tonkinese produced. The physical characteristics are a mixture of these two breeds.

For about ten years breeders in the US and Canada have worked with this breed and it is now accepted for full registration and championship competition in CFF, CCA and ICF. In CFF, application was made in 1974 and through the Tonkinese Breed Club the cat was accepted in 1975. It has been actively bred in this country and in Canada since the early 1960's Among the early breeders one must include Jane Barletta of B'ssa Cattery in New Jersey who began in 1967, Carol Schmidt of Indiana who has been breeding them since 1969 and Margaret Conroy of Ontario, Canada who started in 1965. The first successful breeding program was Margaret Conroy's, and CCA was the first to accept the breed due to her efforts.

Most breeders produced their first generation Tonks from a seal point Siamese bred to a sable Burmese. Other Siamese colors have been experimented with. The breeders feel that the Tonkinese as a new breed stands as half Burmese, half Siamese and thus Tonkinese are bred only to Tonkinese and not back to their parents (to maintain this 50-50 ration). One breeder stated that when she crosses chocolate point Siamese and sable Burmese she gets natural mink Tonkinese. However, if the Burmese has champagne or blue in the background there is a possibility of champagne or blue Tonkinese. The first cross between Siamese and Burmese produces 100% Tonkinese.

Joan Weber's Ch. Blue Su-Lee of Derry Dock, the first blue Tonkinese Champion.

The Tonkinese is friendly and affectionate making an ideal housepet and a beautiful show cat. It is good with children, loving and wants to be near people. It is intelligent, active, curious and playful—always into something. For those interested in knowing more about the Tonkinese or in joining a club there is the CFF affiliated Tonkinese Breed Club. This is an international organization founded by Madalyn Dakin and Judith Penna to promote the breed in the various associations. The club was established in 1974; it has an international membership and publishes a periodic newsletter to advise, counsel and encourage its membership. The newsletter also includes a listing of available studs, kittens and cats for sale.

The Tonkinese is a medium sized cat, well muscled, with hind legs that are slightly higher than the front legs. Its paws are oval and dainty. The mature cat has a rich sound body color shading to a slightly lighter hue on the underside. Its points are a clearly defined darker shading, merged gently into the body color. They come in four colors: natural mink, a rich warm body color with dark chocolate to sable points; honey mink, a warm ruddy brown body color with a slightly reddish cast and points, a rich chocolate brown; champagne, a warm soft beige body color with warm brown points; and blue, a soft blue-gray to medium blue-gray body color with points shading from medium blue-gray to slate. The head should be a modified wedge, a squarish muzzle, with a slight rise from the bridge of the nose to the forehead. The ears are medium in size, softly rounded and pricked forward. The eyes are almond shaped, slightly oriental, set well apart, blue-green in color and gorgeous! The tail is long and tapering, wider at the base than at the tip.

Elaine Gesel's No Ruz Cleopatra, a Turkish Angora kitten. Photo by Chalmer Black.

Turkish Angora

The Turkish Angora, as it is known in this country, originated in Ankara, the capital of Turkey. Angora was the ancient name of this city. Traditionally, the area is known for its longhaired dogs, cats, and goats, this latter from which mohair is provided. The capital city has always had animals and a zoo was established outside the city using local animals. Centuries ago, the Angora moved out of Turkey, became involved with other cats and sooner or later crossed paths with other longhaired cats. This includes the Persian of that time which was quite unlike the Persian of today. It is believed that in its travels the Angora may even have been the first Longhair on American shores. Certain facts about this breed that originated are known today. It is a natural breed, originated in Turkey, lived there centuries ago and lives there today in its natural state. In leaving that country and mixing with other longhaired cats it lost its identity. The Angora as a separate breed disappeared about 1900. Not until the early 1960's in this country did it again regain recognition.

Some others have tried to dispute that there were separate breeds of Longhairs long ago and others came to use the term Angora to mean all longhaired cats. Whatever the origins of other Longhairs at that time, the Angora is a breed unto itself and deserving of its rightful heritage as a natural and separate breed.

References show that people finally took an interest in two specific Longhairs and began to distinguish between the two. Basically these differences could be drawn: the Persian had a round face, short and broad nose, short ears, large and round eyes and a woolly coat which was the same length all over. The Persian's coat also seemed heavier and fuller. The Angora, on the other hand, was a cat with a longer, narrower and more pointed face with a slightly longer nose. The body is cobby and muscular, but larger and longer. The fur is very different. It is shiny, long, very fine and soft and seems to flow. This softer, glossy coat of the Angora is longer in certain areas than in others. Longer fur hangs from the body, the tail, the britches and the ruff around the neck and down the front of the cat while the hair on the main part of the body, back, head and sides lies close to the body. The tail on the two breeds was not the same either. The Persian was said to carry its tail low and level while the Angora carried its tail "gay," high above the body. Obviously, these were two different breeds.

The Turkish word for cat is Kedi and two breeds of cat are recognized in that country. One is the Angora as we know it, which seems to have come from Ankara and lived there for centuries. The other is the Van cat which is a cousin to the Angora but not the same cat at all. The Van cat is found in the eastern section of Turkey in what is called the Van district. These cats are white but have auburn markings particularly on the face and tail and randomly on the body. Little is known of them in the United States

Kenlyn's Kai of No Ruz, a bi-colored black and white male, owned by Elaine Gesel. Breeder was Mrs. Pierce. Photo by Joe Bongi, Jr.

International and Triple Champion No Ruz Sultana, a blue eyed white female owned and bred by Elaine Gesel.

but they are accepted in England as the Turkish cat by the GCCF while the Angora is known simply by that name. Thus the English have managed to breed and accept for show both Turkish breeds. However, in Turkey, they are never mixed and are seen as two separate breeds.

From my information the zoo on the outskirts of Ankara keeps Angoras, but only the white ones. It is true that throughout history references are made to colors in the breed and even in this country Angora clubs are asking registries to accept colors where once they asked only for the white with blue, copper, or odd eyes. However, in Turkey, according to the director of the zoo no colored Angoras are kept. If they appear in litters of white Angoras they are given away. Obviously, the Van cat, with its coloring and status of being a separate breed, is never bred to Angora though the zoo houses a pair of Van cats in addition to Siamese cats, lions, tigers and panthers. The cats are bred once a year. Throughout history, the odd-eyed white always has been the most desirable of the whites. The zoo also keeps records of its litters of Angoras and runs a strict breeding program. This is to insure purity of lines. When they are born, kittens are given an identification number, and the colors of the eyes, sex and birthplace are recorded.

To get a pure Angora in the beginning in this country one had to go to Turkey and that is what Mrs. Liesa F. Grant did in 1962. She purchased a pair from the zoo in Ankara and shipped them to America. The male was an odd-eyed white called Yildiz meaning Star and the female was an amber-eyed white named Yildizcik meaning Starlet. With them came the papers necessary for such imports—bills of sale, certificates of ancestry, injection records and export/import papers. The first litter from this pair was born in 1963. The Grants kept an odd-eyed white male named Mustapha and an amber-eyed white female named Suna Aisha. The original pair were registered with CFA under the Longhair category but in 1968 CFA re-registered all Angora cats under their proper name. The Grants had a problem of inbreeding with only one pair so they returned to Turkey in 1966 and purchased another, unrelated pair. The male was an amber-eyed white named Yaman and the female an odd-eyed white named Marvis. Finally other breeders could get in on this new breed. A kitten from the first pair and one from the second pair were sold to another breeder. The breed was coming of age. Others began importing and breeding the Angora. The Grants showed the Angora to CFA in 1967 and in January 1970 it was recognized. The breed is gaining in popularity and to see grands in this breed class is not unusual. There is no question that it is a natural breed with a heritage all its own.

It is said that this cat loves water and this is especially true of its cousin the Van cat from which, perhaps, it has inherited this trait. A responsive cat, it is very alert and very intelligent. People remark on its adaptability. With ancestors who toured the continents it is no wonder. It is not talkative but is loyal, friendly and very polite. It can be taught tricks, is hardy and has a good life ex-

Hozat of Thornton's Desert, a white male, owned by Mrs. George Thornton. Breeders were Mr. and Mrs. Ivan Leinbach.

Nadja of Thornton's Desert, a female, owned by Mrs. George Thornton. Breeders were Mr. and Mrs. Ivan Leinbach. Photo by Michael Konecky.

Champion No Ruz Shimmer, a blue eyed white, owned and bred by Elaine Gesel. Photo by Chalmer Black.

pectancy. Its love of people, its ease in learning and accepting change make it a joy to own. Without doubt too it is graceful and its movements seem to flow—something an Angora owner is quick to point out.

Known as the Turkish Angora to the show world this cat has a small to medium size, wedge-shaped head wide at the top with a definite taper to the chin. The ears are wide at the base, long, pointed and tufted. They are set high on the head—a distinctive factor. The eyes are large and almond-shaped more round than oriental. The nose is medium long with a gentle slope and no break at all. Its jaw is tapered, its chin gently rounded and its neck slim, graceful and of medium length. The body on this cat is small to medium in the female, larger in the male with a torso that is long, graceful and lithe. The chest is light-framed and the rump is slightly higher than the front of the cat. Basically this is a light-boned cat with long legs, the hind legs being longer than the front ones, and small round paws. The tail is long and tapering, wide at the base, narrow at the end, full and carried lower than the body but not trailing. When the cat is in motion or the tail is relaxed it may be carried horizontally over the body sometimes almost touching the head. The coat on the body is medium long and very long at the ruff. The tail is full and silky with a wavy tendency. The coat is wavier on the stomach but overall it is fine and has a silk-like sheen.

Color Standards

Any of the thirty breeds of cats described in this book may be found at a given point along a cat color spectrum that includes various patterns, color combinations and self colors that have developed as the various breeds developed. In many instances these colors and combinations of colors have been specifically b ed for. Several of the breeds, such as the American Shorthair, the British Shorthair, the Persian, the Manx cat, the Maine Coon cat and others are accepted in most of the same colors. Others are restricted to only one or two colors, such as the singularly colored Burmese, or the Abyssinian and Somali, accepted in the two colors peculiar to these breeds alone. In some, only very specific color combinations are allowable, such as in the Siamese and color-pointed cats.

The following pages contain the color descriptions of the different cat breeds arranged alphabetically by heading to reflect the accepted colors for each. Where colors are unique to only one or two distinct breeds, these color descriptions have been listed by the name of the breed in which they occur. The others are grouped according to the most appropriate color name or pattern.

Abyssinian, Somali

RUDDY: Coat ruddy brown, ticked with various shades of darker brown or black; the extreme outer tip to be the darkest, with orange-brown undercoat, ruddy to the skin. Darker shading along spine allowed if fully ticked. Tail-tipped with black and without rings. The undersides and forelegs (inside) to be a tint to harmonize with the main color. Preference given to unmarked orange-brown (burnt-sienna) color. Nose Leather: tile red. Paw Pads: black or brown, with black between toes and extending slightly beyond the paws. Eye Color: gold or green, the more richness and depth of color the better.

RED: Warm, glowing red, distinctly ticked with chocolate-brown. Deeper shades of red preferred. However, good ticking not to be sacrificed merely for depth of color. Ears and tail tipped with chocolate-brown. Nose Leather: rosy pink. Paw Pads: pink, with chocolate-brown between toes, extending slightly beyond paws. Eye Color: gold or green, the more richness and depth of color the better.

Burmese

SABLE: Mature specimen should be a rich, warm sable-brown. Paw pads and nose leather dark brown. Sable may shade slightly to a lighter tone on chest, abdomen and inside of legs.

CHAMPAGNE: Mature specimen should be a rich, warm honey-beige, shading to a lighter tone on chest, abdomen and inside of legs, with darker shading on face and ears permissible. Paw Pads: warm pinkish. Nose Leather: light, warm brown.

BLUE: Mature specimen should be a rich blue with seasonal fawn overtones. Slightly lighter color allowed on chest, abdomen and inside of legs. Paw Pads and Nose Leather: slate grey with pinkish tinge.

PLATINUM: Mature specimen should be pale, silvery-grey with seasonal fawn overtones. Paw Pads and Nose Leather: lavender-pink.

Cameos

SHELL CAMEO (Red Chinchilla): Undercoat white, the coat on the back, flanks, head and tail to be sufficiently tipped with red to give the characteristic sparkling appearance. Face and legs may be very slightly shaded with tipping. Chin, ear tufts, stomach and chest white. Nose Leather: rose. Rims of Eyes: rose. Paw Pads: rose. Eye Color: brilliant gold.

SHADED CAMEO (Red Shaded): Undercoat white with a mantle of red tipping shading down the sides, face, and tail from dark on the ridge to white on the chin, chest, stomach, and under the tail. Legs to be the same tone as face. The general effect to be much redder than the Shell Cameo. Nose Leather: rose. Rims of Eyes: rose. Paw Pads: rose. Eye Color: brilliant gold.

Egyptian Mau

SILVER: Pale silver ground color across the head, shoulders, outer legs, back, and tail. Underside fades to a brilliant pale silver. All markings charcoal color, showing good contrast against lighter ground colors. Back of ears greyish-pink and tipped in black. Nose, lips, and eyes outlined in black. Upper throat area, chin and around nostrils pale clear silver, appearing white. Nose Leather: brick red. Paw Pads: black, with black between the toes and extending beyond the paws of the hind legs.

BRONZE: Light bronze ground color across head, shoulders, outer legs, back and tail, being darkest on the saddle and lightening to a tawny-buff on the sides. Underside fades to a creamy ivory. All markings dark brown, showing good contrast against the lighter ground color. Back of ears tawny-pink and tipped in dark brown. Nose, lips, and eyes outlined in dark brown, with bridge of nose ocherous. Upper throat area, chin, and around nostrils pale creamy white. Nose Leather: brick red. Paw Pads: black or dark brown, with same color between toes and extending beyond the paws of the hind legs.

SMOKE: Charcoal grey color with silver undercoat across head, shoulders, legs, tail and underside. All markings jet black, with sufficient contrast against ground color for pattern to be plainly visible. Nose, lips, and eyes outlined in jet black. Upper throat area, chin, and around nostrils lightest in color. Nose Leather:

black. Paw Pads: black with black between the toes and extending beyond the paws of the hind legs.

PEWTER: Ground color suggesting pale fawn. Each hair to be composed of bands of pale silver and beige with black tipping. Loses ticking and lightens to cream on undersides. Chin, upper throat and nose outlined in cream. Markings charcoal to dark brown, with good contrast between ground color and markings. Paw Pads: charcoal to dark brown. Nose Leather: brick red. Eyes, nose and lips outlined in charcoal to dark brown.

Japanese Bobtail

WHITE: Pure glistening white.

BLACK: Dense, coal black, sound from roots to tip of fur. Shiny and free from any tinge of rust on tips.

RED: Deep, rich, clear, brilliant red, the deeper and more glowing in tone the better.

BLACK AND WHITE, RED AND WHITE.

MI-KE (Tri-Color): Black, red, and white, or tortoiseshell with white.

TORTOISESHELL: Black, red, and cream.

OTHER JAPANESE BOBTAIL COLORS (OJBC) include the following categories and any other color or pattern or combination thereof except coloring that is point-restricted (i.e., Siamese markings) or unpatterned agouti (i.e., Abyssinian coloring). Patterned categories denote and include any variety of tabby striping or spotting with or without areas of solid (unmarked) color, with preference given to bold, dramatic markings and rich, vivid coloring.

OTHER SOLID COLORS: Blue or cream. Patterned self-colors: Red, black, blue, cream, silver or brown. Other bi-colors: blue and white or cream and white. Patterned bi-colors: red, black, blue, cream, silver, or brown, combined with white. Patterned tortoiseshell. Blue-cream. Patterned blue-cream. Dilute tri-colors: Blue, cream, and white. Patterned dilute tri-colors. Patterned Mi-Ke (tri-color).

Particolors

TORTOISESHELL: Black with unbrindled patches of red and cream. Patches clearly defined and well broken on both body and extremities. Blaze of red or cream on face is desirable. Eye Color: brilliant gold.

CALICO: White with unbrindled patches of black and red. White predominant on underparts. Eye Color: brilliant gold.

DILUTE CALICO: White with unbrindled patches of blue and cream. White predominant on underparts. Eye Color: brilliant gold.

BLUE-CREAM: Blue with patches of solid cream. Patches clearly defined and well broken on both body and extremities. Eye Color: brilliant gold.

BI-COLOR: White with unbrindled patches of black, or white with unbrindled patches of blue, or white with unbrindled patches of red, or white with unbrindled patches of cream. Eye Color: gold, the more brilliant the better.

TORTOISESHELL WITH WHITE: Color as defined for Tortoiseshell with or without white on the face. Must have white on bib, belly and all four paws. White on one-third of body is desirable.

CHESTNUT-TORTIE: Chestnut brown with unbrindled patches of red and cream. Patches clearly defined and well broken on both body and extremities. Blaze of red or cream on face is desirable.

LAVENDER-CREAM: Lavender with patches of solid cream. Patches clearly defined and well broken on both the body and extremities.

Pointed Cats

RED POINT: Body clear white with any shading in the same tone as points. Points: deep red. Nose Leather: flesh or coral pink. Paw Pads: flesh or coral pink. Eye Color: deep vivid blue.

CREAM POINT: Body clear white with any shading in the same tone as points. Points: apricot. Nose Leather: flesh to coral pink. Paw Pads: flesh to coral pink. Eye Color: deep vivid blue.

SEAL-TORTIE POINT: Body pale fawn to cream, shading to lighter color on stomach and chest. Body color is mottled with cream in older cats. Points: seal brown, uniformly mottled with red and cream; a blaze is desirable. Nose Leather: seal brown to match point color; flesh or coral pink mottling permitted where there is a blaze. Paw Pads: seal brown to match point color; flesh or coral pink mottling permitted where the point color mottling extends into the paw pads. Eye Color: deep vivid blue.

CHOCOLATE-CREAM POINT: Body ivory, mottled in older cats. Points: warm milk-chocolate uniformly mottled with cream; a blaze is desirable. Nose Leather: cinnamon; flesh or coral pink mottling permitted where there is a blaze. Paw Pads: cinnamon; flesh or coral pink mottling permitted where the point color mottling extends into the paw pads. Eye Color: deep vivid blue.

BLUE-CREAM POINT: Body bluish white to platinum grey, cold in tone, shading to lighter color on stomach and chest. Body color is mottled in older cats. Points: deep blue-grey uniformly mottled with cream; a blaze is desirable. Nose Leather: slate-colored; flesh or coral pink mottling permitted where there is a blaze. Paw Pads: slate-colored; flesh or coral pink mottling permitted where the point color mottling extends into the paw pads. Eye Color: deep vivid blue.

LILAC-CREAM POINT: Body glacial white, mottling if any in the shade of the points. Points: frosty grey with pinkish tone, uniformly mottled with pale cream; a blaze is desirable. Nose Leather: lavender-pink; flesh or coral pink mottling permitted where there is a blaze. Paw Pads: lavender-pink; flesh or coral pink mottling permitted where the point color mottling extends into the paw pads. Eye Color: deep vivid blue.

RED-LYNX POINT: Body white. Body shading may take form of ghost striping. Points: deep red bars, distinct and separated by lighter background color; ears deep red, paler thumbprint in center. Nose Leather: flesh or coral pink. Paw Pads: flesh or coral pink. Eye Color: deep vivid blue.

SEAL-LYNX POINT: Body cream or pale fawn, shading to lighter color on stomach and chest. Body shading may take form of ghost striping. Points: seal brown bars, distinct and separated by lighter background color; ears seal brown with paler thumbprint in center. Nose Leather: seal brown or pink edged in seal brown. Paw Pads: seal brown. Eye Color: deep vivid blue.

CHOCOLATE-LYNX POINT: Body ivory. Body shading may take form of ghost striping. Points: warm milk-chocolate bars, distinct and separated by lighter background color; ears warm milk-chocolate with paler thumbprint in center. Nose Leather: cinnamon or pink edged in cinnamon. Paw Pads: cinnamon. Eye Color: deep vivid blue.

BLUE-LYNX POINT: Body bluish white to platinum grey, cold in tone, shading to lighter color on stomach and chest. Body shading may take form of ghost striping. Points: deep blue-grey bars, distinct and separated by lighter background color; ears deep blue-grey with paler thumbprints in center. Nose Leather: slate-colored or pink edged in slate. Paw Pads: slate-colored. Eye Color: deep vivid blue.

LILAC-LYNX POINT: Body glacial white. Body shading may take form of ghost striping. Points: frosty grey with pinkish tone bars, distinct and separated by lighter background color; ears frosty grey with pinkish tone, paler thumbprint in center. Nose Leather: lavender-pink or pink edged in lavender-pink. Paw Pads: lavender-pink. Eye Color: deep vivid blue.

SEAL POINT: Body even pale fawn to cream, warm in tone, shading gradually to lighter color on the stomach and chest. Points, except for gloves, deep seal brown. Gloves pure white. Nose Leather: same color as the points. Paw Pads: pink. Eye Color: blue, the deeper and more violet the better.

BLUE POINT: Body bluish white, cold in tone, shading gradually to almost white on stomach and chest. Points, except for gloves on paws, deep blue. Gloves pure white. Nose Leather: slate-color. Paw Pads: pink. Eye Color: blue, the deeper and more violet the better.

CHOCOLATE POINT: Body ivory with no shading. Points, except for gloves on paws, milk-chocolate color, warm in tone. Gloves pure white. Nose Leather: cinnamon-pink. Paw Pads: pink. Eye Color: Blue, the deeper and more violet the better.

LILAC POINT: Body a cold, glacial tone verging on white with no shading. Points, except for gloves, frosty grey with pinkish tone. Gloves pure white. Nose Leather: lavender-pink. Paw Pads: pink. Eye Color: blue, the deeper and more violet the better.

FLAME POINT: Body creamy white. Points delicate orange flame. Nose Leather: flesh or coral pink. Paw Pads: flesh or coral pink. Eye Color: deep vivid blue.

TORTIE POINT: Body creamy white or pale fawn. Points seal with unbrindled patches of red and cream. Blaze of red or cream on face is desirable. Nose Leather: seal brown with flesh and/or coral pink mottling to conform with colors of points. Eye Color: deep vivid blue.

BLUE-CREAM POINT: Body bluish white or creamy white, shading gradually to white on the stomach and chest. Points: blue with patches of cream. Nose Leather: slate blue, pink, or a combination of slate blue and pink. Paw Pads: slate blue, pink, or a combination of slate blue and pink. Eye Color: deep vivid blue.

Silvers

CHINCHILLA: Undercoat pure white. Coat on back, flanks, head and tail sufficiently tipped with black to give the characteristic sparkling silver appearance. Legs may be slightly shaded with tipping. Chin and ear tufts, stomach and chest, pure white. Rims of eyes, lips and nose outlined with black. Nose leather: brick red. Paw Pads: black. Eye Color: green or blue-green.

SHADED SILVER: Undercoat white with a mantle of black tipping shading down from sides, face and tail from dark on the ridge to white on the chin, chest, stomach and under the tail. Legs to be the same tone as the face. The general effect to be much darker than a chinchilla. Rims of eyes, lips and nose outlined with black. Nose Leather: brick red. Paw Pads: black. Eye Color: green or blue-green.

CHINCHILLA GOLDEN: A white cat with flanks, head, ears and tail lightly tipped with brown to give the characteristic sparkling golden appearance. Chin, ear tufts, stomach and chest pure white. Rims of eyes, lips and nose outlined with brown. Paw Pads: black. Center of nose brick red. Eyes: orange. Undesirable: dark spots, shading, barring, or brown or cream tinge.

Smokes

BLACK SMOKE: White undercoat, deeply tipped with black. Cat in repose appears black. In motion the white undercoat is clearly apparent. Points and mask black with narow band of white at base of hairs next to skin which may be seen only when the fur is parted. Nose Leather: black. Paw Pads: black. Eye Color: brilliant gold.

BLUE SMOKE: White undercoat, deeply tipped with blue. Cat in repose appears blue. In motion the white undercoat is clearly apparent. Points and mask blue, with narrow band of white at base of hairs next to skin which may be seen only when fur is parted. Nose Leather: blue. Paw Pads: blue. Eye Color: brilliant gold.

CAMEO SMOKE (Red Smoke): White undercoat, deeply tipped with red. Cat in repose appears red. In motion the white undercoat is clearly apparent. Points and mask red with narrow band of white at base of hairs next to skin, which may be seen only when fur is parted. Nose Leather: rose. Rims of Eyes: rose. Paw Pads: rose. Eye Color: brilliant gold.

CHESTNUT SMOKE: White undercoat, deeply tipped with brown. Cat in repose appears brown. In motion the white undercoat is clearly apparent. Points and mask brown, with narrow band of white at base of hairs next to skin which may be seen only when fur is parted. Nose Leather: pinkish shade. Paw Pads: pinkish shade.

LAVENDER SMOKE: White undercoat, deeply tipped with lavender. Cat in repose appears lavender. In motion the white undercoat is clearly apparent. Points and mask lavender with narrow band of white at base of hairs next to skin which may be seen only when fur is parted. Nose Leather: lavender pink. Paw Pads: lavender pink.

EBONY SMOKE: White undercoat, deeply tipped with black. Cat in repose appears black. In motion the white undercoat is clearly apparent. Points and mask black with narrow band of white at base of hairs next to skin which may be seen only when the fur is parted. Nose Leather: black. Paw Pads: black.

TORTOISESHELL SMOKE: (Smoke Tortoiseshell or Cameo Tortoiseshell) The three colors of black red and cream shall conform to the Tortoiseshell pattern with a white undercoat. Mask and feet conform to the Tortoiseshell standard. White frill and ear tufts. Eyes copper. Paw Pads and Nose Leather may be patched in charcoal, rose or pink.

SHADED BLUE CREAM CAMEO: Tipping to be in well-defined patches of blue and cream, resembling the Blue Cream Standard, except for the tipping (cameo effect). Undercoat to be clear silvery-white. Cream tipping should be present on face, flanks, back, toes and tail. Blaze on face is desirable. Objections: Tabby markings, brindling, solid blue or solid cream tipping on face or tail.

Solid Colors

WHITE: Pure glistening white. Nose Leather: pink. Paw Pads: pink. Eye Color: deep blue or brilliant gold. Odd-eyed whites shall have one blue and one gold eye with equal color depth.

BLACK: Dense coal black, sound from roots to tip of fur. Free from any tinge of rust on tips or smoke undercoat. Nose Leather: black. Paw Pads: black or brown. Eye Color: brilliant gold.

BLUE: Blue, lighter shade preferred, one level tone from nose to tip of tail. Sound to the roots. A sound darker shade is more acceptable than an unsound lighter shade. Nose Leather: blue. Paw Pads: blue. Eye Color: brilliant gold.

RED: Deep, rich, clear, brilliant red; without shading, markings or ticking. Lips and chin the same color as coat. Nose Leather: brick red. Paw Pads: brick red. Eye Color: brilliant gold.

CREAM: One level shade of buff cream, without markings. Sound to the roots. Lighter shades preferred. Nose Leather: pink. Paw Pads: pink. Eye Color: brilliant gold.

CHESTNUT: Rich chestnut brown, sound throughout. Whiskers and nose leather same color as coat. Paw Pads: pinkish shade.

LAVENDER: Frost-grey with a pinkish tone, sound and even throughtout. Nose Leather and Paw Pads: lavender pink.

EBONY: Dense coal black, sound from roots to tip of fur. Free from any tinge of rust on tips or smoke undercoat. Nose Leather: black. Paw Pads: black or brown.

PEKE-FACE RED, PEKE-FACE RED TABBY: The Peke Face cat should conform in color, markings and general type to the standards set forth for the red and red tabby Persian cat. The head should resemble as much as possible that of the Pekinese dog from which it gets its name. Nose should be very short and depressed, or indented between the eyes. There should be a decidedly wrinkled muzzle. Eyes round, large, and full, set wide apart, prominent and brilliant.

CHOCOLATE: Warm, rich chocolate. Eyes: copper preferable, but paler color acceptable. (Deduct full 10 points for blue or green eyes). Paw Pads and Nose Leather: chocolate brown, pink cast allowed. Undesirable: shading, barring or light spots.

LILAC: Clear, uniform lilac with mauve (pink-brown) cast. Eyes copper, but paler color acceptable. Paw Pads and Nose Leather: brown with pinkish tinge.

Tabby

CLASSIC TABBY PATTERN: Markings dense, clearly defined and broad. Legs evenly barred with bracelets coming up to meet the body markings. Tail evenly ringed. Several unbroken necklaces on neck and upper chest, the more the better. Frown marks on forehead form intricate letter "M." Unbroken line runs back from outer corner of eye. Swirls on cheeks. Vertical lines over back of head extend to shoulder markings which are in the shape of a butterfly with both upper and lower wings distinctly outlined and marked with dots inside outline. Back markings consist of a vertical line down the spine from butterfly to tail with a vertical stripe paralleling it on each side, the three stripes well separated by stripes of the ground color. Large solid blotch on each side to be encircled by one or more unbroken rings. Side markings should be the same on both sides. Double vertical row of buttons on chest and stomach.

MACKEREL TABBY PATTERN: Markings dense, clearly defined, and all narrow pencillings. Legs evenly barred with narrow bracelets coming up to meet the body markings. Tail barred. Necklaces on neck and chest distinct, like so many chains. Head barred with an "M" on the forehead. Unbroken lines running back from the eyes. Lines running down the head to meet the shoulders. Spine lines run together to form a narrow saddle. Narrow pencillings run around body.

SPOTTED TABBY PATTERN: Markings on the body to be spotted. May vary in size and shape with preference given to round evenly distributed spots. Spots should not run together in a broken Mackerel pattern. A dorsal stripe runs the length of the body to the tip of the tail. The stripe is ideally composed of spots. The markings of the face and forehead shall be typically tabby markings, underside of the body to have "vest buttons." Legs and tail are barred. Nose Leather: pink rimmed with marking color.

TICKED TABBY PATTERN: Body hairs to be ticked with various shades of marking color and ground color. Body when viewed from top to be free from noticeable spots, stripes, or blotches, except for darker dorsal shading. Lighter underside may show tabby markings. Face, legs, and tail must show distinct tabby striping. Cat must have at least one distinct necklace.

SILVER TABBY: Ground color, including lips and chin, pale, clear silver. Markings dense black. Nose Leather: brick red. Paw Pads: black. Eye Color: green or Hazel.

RED TABBY: Ground color red. Markings deep, rich red. Lips and chin red. Nose Leather: brick red. Paw Pads: brick red. Eye Color: brilliant gold.

BROWN TABBY: Ground color brilliant coppery brown. Markings dense black. Lips and chin the same shades as the rings around the eyes. Back of leg black from paw to heel. Nose Leather: brick red. Paw Pads: black or brown. Eye Color: brilliant gold.

BLUE TABBY: Ground color, including lips and chin, pale bluish ivory. Markings a very deep blue affording a good contrast with gound color. Warm fawn overtones or patina over the whole. Nose Leather: old rose. Paw Pads: rose. Eye Color: brilliant gold.

CREAM TABBY: Ground color, including lips and chin, very pale cream. Markings of buff or cream sufficiently darker than the ground color to afford good contrast, but remaining within the dilute color range. Nose Leather: pink. Paw Pads: pink. Eye Color: brilliant gold.

CAMEO TABBY: Ground color off-white. Markings red. Nose Leather: rose. Paw Pads: rose. Eye Color: brilliant gold.

EBONY TABBY: Ground color brilliant coppery brown. Markings dense black. Lips and chin the same shades as the rings around the eyes. Back of leg black from paw to heel. Nose Leather: brick red. Paw Pads: black or brown.

CHESTNUT TABBY: Ground color is warm fawn, markings are bright chestnut. Nose Leather, chestnut. Paw Pads: chestnut.

LAVENDER TABBY: Ground color is pale lavender. Markings are rich lavender affording a good contrast with the ground color. Nose Leather: lavender pink. Paw Pads: lavender pink.

ORC (Other Rex Colors) : Any other color or pattern with the exeption of those showing hybridization resulting in the colors chocolate, lavender, the Himalayan pattern, or these combinations with white, etc. Eye Color: appropriate to the predominant color of the cat.

OMC (Other Manx Colors) : Any other color or pattern with the exception of those showing hybridization resulting in the colors chocolate, lavender, the Himalayan pattern, or these combinations with white, etc. Eye Color: appropriate to the predominat color of the coat.

Tonkinese

NATURAL MINK: Body a rich warm brown color. Points, a dark chocolate to sable. Leather: dark brown.

HONEY MINK: Body a warm ruddy brown with a reddish cast. Points, a rich chocolate brown. Leather: medium dark brown.

CHAMPAGNE: Colors to be a soft warm beige. Gradual darkening in older cats. Points to be warm light brown. Leather to be pink to cinnamon. Objections: lack of definite leg gauntlets; win withheld.

BLUE: Body to vary from a soft blue grey to medium blue grey. Points, a medium blue to slate. Leather: blue grey. Objections: lack of definite leg gauntlets; win withheld.

Index

Simpson, Frances, 193
Smith, Helen, 40, 41
Smokeyhill Cattery, 52
Smokes (Color Standards), 343
Solid Colors (Color Standards), 344
Somali (Color Standard), 335
Speaking Balinese, 44
Stirling-Webb, Brian A., 139, 140, 259
Swiss Mountain Cat, 135

T
Tabby (Color Standards), 346
Temple of Lao-Tsun, 47
Thompson, Dr. Joseph, 99
Ti-Mau Cattery, 41
Todd, Dr. Neil, 198, 271, 272
Tonkinese (Color Standards), 348
Tonkinese Breed Club, 323, 324
Troubetskoye, Natalie, 121, 122
Turner, Patricia, 210, 271

U
United Abyssinian Club, 11
Universal Dictionary of Commerce, of Natural History and of the Arts and Trades, 107

V
Verde Cattery, 41
von Ullman, Baroness, 135, 210

W
Whittemore, Mrs. Robert, 193
Woodiwiss, Major Sydney, 15, 16
Wyola Cattery, 271, 272

Y
Young, Donald and Elaine, 41, 43

Z
Zanetti, Aida, 11